Prophecy

Prophecy

*exercising the prophetic gifts of
the Spirit in the church today*

Bruce Yocum

Servant Books
Ann Arbor, Michigan

Published by: Servant Books
                  Box 8617
                  Ann Arbor, Michigan 48107

ISBN 0-89283-029-8

Printed in the United States of America

Contents

Acknowledgements

I would like to express my thanks to at least some of the very many people who helped me with the writing of this book. Rev. George Montague, Rev. Salvador Carillo Alday, Rev. Paul LeBeau, and Dr. Kevin Ranaghan took time in their very busy schedules to make many helpful comments and suggestions. Mr. and Mrs. Thomas Adams' characteristic generosity provided the seculsion necessary for completing the task. John Keating and Mark Kinzer provided excellent assistance with research and writing. Most of all, Bert Ghezzi, Nick Cavnar, and Vicki Forrester, who perhaps labored on this book as much as the author, deserve my gratitude. Finally, my secretary, Alice Rock, assisted in numerous helpful and thoughtful ways. May God bless all of you.

Preface

This work grew out of experience, and reflection upon Scripture and the early church documents. It is not possible to distinguish, in most cases, whether a passage from Scripture was illuminated by experience, or whether the testimony of the Scriptures opened us to new experience. But we are convinced that our own experience of prophecy is in harmony with the experience of the first Christians, and that it is an experience which God wishes to bestow widely upon his people.

The book is divided into two distinct sections. In the first, we focus upon the "normal" experience of Christian prophecy, that is, the experience which ought to be normative for us. In the second, we focus on the actual current experience of most of those who have begun to be familiar with prophecy. We have not yet attained to the norm. It is our hope that these reflections will contribute to the realization of that norm. The wish Moses expressed for the people of Israel can still express our wish for Christians today:

If only the whole people of Yahweh were prophets, and Yahweh gave his spirit to them all.

(Num. 11:29)

Bruce Yocum

Introduction

The church was dark and very quiet at 5 a.m., and I felt small amidst the rows and rows of empty pews. I was the altar boy assigned to the 5:30 a.m. mass, and I had come early just so I could pray. I was impressed by my holiness. Not many people come to church that early just to pray, I thought; certainly not many ten year old boys. My conviction that I was doing something quite unusual had been confirmed by the police officers who had stopped me three blocks from the church. They were openly skeptical when I told them why I was out on the streets at that hour of the morning. They drove me right to the door of the church to be sure I actually went inside.

I had grown up on stories of the saints: saints who fasted and worked miracles, converted hundreds of pagans, conquered temptations and spent long hours in prayer. Saints, of course, also got up very early in the morning to pray. As I sat there in the church considering all this, it suddenly occurred to me that I had to pray. Even I knew that it wasn't holy just to get up at 5 a.m.; it was only holy if you did it to pray. So I set about praying.

I was not a very accomplished prayer. The first few minutes were spent noticing all of the funny little noises in the darkened church. Then I remembered what one of the nuns had taught me. "Just talk to God," she said, "the same way you would talk to a friend."

"O God, I love you."

My heart almost stopped as my words, spoken aloud, echoed back to me from around the church. I was ashamed at how much the noise had startled me. I began again, this time prepared for the noise.

"O God, I want to love you and do whatever is right."

After those words I fell silent, not through fear of the noise I had made, but through amazement at what I had heard in my heart. *I heard God speaking to me!* I heard the voice of God—not with my bodily ears, but in the quietness of my heart—telling me of the love that he had for me. I felt his love surrounding me, holding me.

A moment or two later I opened my eyes, brushed away my tears, and looked around. Everything seemed so normal, I wondered if I had just fallen asleep or started imagining things. But I knew that I had neither dreamt nor fantasized. God had spoken to me.

Ten years later I walked into the second story apartment of some recent acquaintances. I was now a sophomore in college, and still wanted to know God, though I am afraid I knew him little better at twenty than I had at ten. There were perhaps fifteen people gathered in the living room, and they welcomed me with a warmth which surprised me. I felt a little uncomfortable; I had come to the apartment to pray with them (they said they got together regularly to pray), and I had no idea what they did when they prayed.

Several others arrived in the next few minutes, and then we began to pray. Several songs, two or three Scripture passages and a few minutes of quiet praying later, I was starting to feel more at home. Suddenly, the man seated next to me began speaking:

I am your Lord, and I love you with a perfect love. Set your hearts on me and on my kingdom.

He spoke in the first person, as had the prophets in the Old Testament. He spoke as if God himself were speaking to us. And I believed that it was God. I was gripped by the same conviction that I had experienced ten years earlier: God had spoken to me.

God has an intense desire to speak to his people. Over and over again in both the Old and the New Testament, God addresses himself to his people, revealing his eagerness to be known by them. A story in the first chapter of the Second Book of Kings (v. 1-4) illustrates God's willingness to speak to us. The king of Israel had fallen from a roof terrace in his palace and had been seriously injured. He wished to know if he would live or die, so he sent messengers to the shrine of Baalzebub, the god of Ekron, to inquire of the god about his fate. But the messengers were intercepted by the prophet Elijah. Through Elijah, God sent a message back to the king: "Is it because there is no God in Israel that you are sending to the god of Ekron?" God was angry with the king. Surely the king should have known how much his God wished to speak with him. He did not need to go somewhere else for an answer.

Yet over and over again God's people show that they do not believe God will speak to them. Today, Christians will consult experts and hold discussions and talk over alternatives before making a decision. But how often will they seriously ask God for the answer they need?

If you do not believe that God is willing to speak to us, then you do not understand God. All through the Scriptures God tells us that he desires to speak ever more intimately, ever more frequently with those who follow him. He uses images of deep intimacy to describe his relationship with his people: he is their husband, their father, their mother, their shepherd. God never wants to be more distant from his people—he wants to be closer to them.

In the times of the Old Covenant, God frequently sent prophets to his people to let them know his word and to guide them into his ways. And he spoke of the day when he would reveal himself even more completely, when the knowledge of God would fill the earth as the waters cover the sea (Isa. 11:9). In the New Testament, with the coming of Jesus, that amazing promise was fulfilled. Do you know what that means? God himself now lives in every man who follows Jesus, drawing every man into a closer, more intimate, more perfect oneness with himself. Among many other things that means that every Christian can hear God speaking to him.

I have a friend, Gerry, who ten years ago learned that God could speak to him personally and directly. Gerry had been raised as a Christian and had believed in God all his life; in fact, following God was the most important thing in his life. But like many Christians, he did not really know God directly. He knew a lot *about* God and what God was like, but he did not have a direct and personal knowledge of God. During college Gerry got involved with a group of other Christians who took their Christian commitment as seriously as he did. The group met together regularly to talk about living as Christians and growing in the Christian life. A member of that group once told Gerry, "When you pray, you shouldn't spend all of the time speaking to God. You should give the Lord some time to speak to you." He said that God would speak to us, actually say something to a person directly.

Well, Gerry filed that one away with all the other interesting things he could think about some day. He did not spend any time when he prayed waiting for the Lord to speak to him because he just didn't believe it would happen. The following summer, however, things changed. One day the advice his friend had given came back to mind: "Give the Lord some time to speak to you."

He decided to try it. He sat back and cleared his mind of all the wandering thoughts and daydreams that seemed to fill it whenever he wanted to pray, then waited for the Lord to speak. Now Gerry didn't have a lot of faith that this would work. In fact, he expected to sit there for a few minutes doing nothing, and then get up and go about the business of the day with another item on his list of things that didn't work in prayer. But that's not what happened.

As soon as he put aside his distractions and tried to hear the Lord, Gerry heard God speak.

"I expected to be kneeling there in silence, with only the walls of the room for company. But as soon as my mind was cleared, I was shocked by an awareness that Jesus was present. I don't mean that I saw a figure or heard sounds, but I knew that Jesus was there; it was as if he were across the room from me with his arms outstretched, crying and saying, 'Come to me.'

"I was totally surprised. For one thing, I hadn't really expected anything to happen, and here was the Lord himself before me. But also, he was saying 'come to me' in a way which clearly showed he felt there was some distance between us. I had been seeing our relationship very differently: I thought that everything between me and the Lord looked fine—even that he should be happy to have me on his side. After a puzzled pause, I said, 'I love you, Lord. What more do you want?'

"Immediately, I knew his answer, I had made myself more important than the Lord, to the point that I had felt he should be thankful for my love. Instead, I should have been at the Lord's feet, thanking him for loving and saving me. I changed my attitude at that moment, and immediately I came close to him."

Gerry came that day to a direct and personal knowledge of God. His knowledge of God has endured and grown, because that day was only a beginning. That was the day Gerry learned that God would speak to him and God has spoken to him many times since.

Gerry is not a "mystic"; he is a Christian. It is not only very special people who get to hear God speak. Every Christian can know God in a direct and personal way and can hear the Lord speaking to him.

I know a great many Christians who believe that God wants them to know and follow his will. On that score they show that they know something about God. But many of them lack faith that God will let them know clearly what his will is. In other words, they believe that God *requires them to do something,* but they do not believe that he will also *provide what they need to do it.* Knowing God's will becomes for such Christians a test or a trial: "God will bless me if I am holy enough or clever enough or lucky enought to discover his will for me." When approached in this way, finding God's direction for your life is like trying to find the hidden object in a picture puzzle: it is possible, but not easy.

God did not try to hide his will from the king of Israel; in fact he was eager to reveal it. But the king did not ask God for direction. His actions betrayed the level of his faith and the depth of his knowledge of God. We do the very same thing in our own lives. When we want to know what we should do or what will happen in our lives, we may study and think and ask advice. But we don't ask God. Of course when we have to make decisions it is right to study and to think and to ask advice, but it is even more right for us to ask God. "Is it because there is no God in Israel" that we ask everywhere else? The way in which we seek guidance or direction for our lives will reveal something about our level of faith and the depth of our knowledge of God.

This book is about one way in which God speaks to us: the gift of prophecy. It is different from many books about prophecy; it does not speak so much *about* prophets as it speaks to prophets. This book is an attempt to help people learn how to open themselves up to the prophetic workings of the Holy Spirit. In one sense it is a manual on "How to Be a Prophet." Of course, no one can decide to be a prophet; the decision lies with God. But God *does* decide that many of his people should be prophets. And once God has given the gift, the person who receives it should learn how to exercise that gift well.

It is my hope that this book will help prophets learn to serve and glorify God with the gift which God has assigned them, and that it will help us all to understand, receive, and support the prophetic gift which God has poured out upon the church.

I

The Role of the Prophet in the Church

The intention of this section is to describe how prophecy functioned in the early church, and how it ought to function today. This is not a picture of how prophecy is being exercised today, but of how it should be exercised. The material for this section is drawn from Scripture, early church writings and contemporary experience. The goal is to present a clear understanding of how God intends prophecy to function among Christians.

Chapter One

A Brief History of Christian Prophecy

When most Christians think of prophecy, they have in mind the great prophets of the Old Testament: Isaiah, Jeremiah, Ezekiel, and the rest. In fact, most Christians probably think of prophecy only as an Old Testament phenomenon. Yet the pages of the New Testament are filled with the influence, the words, and even the names of the prophets who lived after the death of Jesus. The Acts of the Apostles alone records at least five instances of prophetic actions.

The first instance occurs in Acts chapter eleven. A prophet named Agabus, speaking under the inspiration of the Holy Spirit, predicted that a famine would soon come to the whole world. The writer of Acts mentions that this famine did in fact take place during the reign of the emperor Claudius. The prophetic revelation given through Agabus enabled the early Christians to prepare for the disaster in plenty of time.

Somewhat later we read of the decision made at Antioch to send out Barnabas and Paul as missioners (Acts 13:1-4). As the leaders of the church, among whom were prophets, prayed together, the Holy Spirit spoke to confirm their decision to send out the two men.

The fifteenth chapter of Acts mentions two men, Judas and Silas, "who were themselves prophets." They encouraged and strengthened the disciples at Antioch through an inspired discourse. And finally, in the twenty-first chapter, we read these accounts of prophets warning Paul of the dangers that would face him in Jerusalem:

> We looked for the disciples and stayed with them for a week. Under the Spirit's prompting, they tried to tell Paul that he should not go up to Jerusalem; but to no purpose.
>
> (Acts 21:4ff.)

> This man had four unmarried daughters, gifted with prophecy. During our few days stay, a prophet named Agabus arrived from Judea. He came up to us and taking Paul's belt, tied his own hands and feet with it. Then he said, "Thus says the Holy Spirit: This is how the Jews in Jerusalem will bind the owner of this belt and hand him over to the gentiles."
>
> (Acts 21:9ff.)

The early Christians prophesied regularly when they met together (1 Cor. 11:4-5, 14:3 pass.); converts prophesied at the laying on of hands (Acts 19:6); prophecy is listed frequently as one of the gifts Christ bestows upon the church (Rom. 12:6; Eph. 4:11-12; 1 Cor. 12:10, 28, 29); prophets are a part of the foundation of the church (Eph. 2:20); it was to the apostles and the prophets that the revelation of the full plan of salvation was given (Eph. 3:4-6); prophets are mentioned in connection with the ministry of Timothy (1 Tim. 1:18, 4:14); Christians are encouraged to value prophecy (1 Thess. 5:20) and to seek it more earnestly than the other gifts (1 Cor. 14:1). Christian prophets emerge from the pages of the New Testamen as a major element in the church.

The record of prophetic activity extends well beyond the New Testament. The *Didache,* a church manual from the early second century, makes several references to prophets. Its instruction on how to relate to prophets speaks clearly of the presence of prophetic activity. Later, about the year 162, the Christian apologist Justin mentions prophecy in a dialogue with a Jewish rabbi, the *Dialogue With Trypho.* He points to the gift as part of his evidence for the truth of Christianity:

> From the fact that even to this day the gifts of prophecy exist among us Christians, you should realize that the gifts which had resided among your people have now been transferred to us.[1]

Similarly, Irenaeus of Lyons speaks in the late second century of the presence of the gift of prophecy among Christians:

> For this reason does the apostle declare, "We speak wisdom among the mature," terming those persons "mature" who have received the Spirit of God and through the Spirit of God do speak in all languages, as he himself also spoke. In like manner we do also hear many brothers in the Church who possess prophetic gifts, and bring to light for the general benefit the hidden things of men . . . [2]

We even have a prophecy recorded from the late second century. Melito, bishop of Sardis and a renowned holy man, preached a famous sermon *On the Pasch.* At the end of the sermon he broke into prophecy:

> Who will contend against me: Let him stand before me.
> It is I who delivered the condemned. It is I who gave life to the dead.

It is I who raised up the buried. Who will argue with me?
It is I, says Christ who destroyed death. It is I who
triumphed over the enemy,
And trod down Hades, and bound the strong man,
And have snatched mankind up to the heights of heaven.
It is I says Christ.
So then come here all you families of men, weighed down
by your sins
And receive pardon for your misdeeds. For I am your
pardon.
I am the passover which brings salvation. I am the lamb
slain for you.
I am your lustral bath. I am your life. I am your resurrec-
tion.
I am your light, I am your salvation, I am your king.
It is I who bring you up to the heights of heaven.
It is I who give you resurrection there.
I will show you the eternal Father. I will raise you up with
my own right hand.[3]

Prophecy Since the Third Century

It is clear that since the third century prophecy has been
neither continuously manifest in the church, nor common to
the whole church at any one time. There have been, however,
regular recurrences of prophetic activity in the history of the
church, most commonly in certain movements of renewal. In
such movements, prophecy did not occur as an isolated
spiritual phenomenon, but rather as an element of a broader
manifestation of "charismatic" power. Healings, miracles, inspired preaching and other "charisms" were all witnessed by
the participants in these renewal movements.

The first, and most outstanding, of these movements was
the ascetic movement which swept through the church, par-

ticularly in Egypt and Asia Minor, during the fourth, fifth and sixth centuries. There are numerous accounts of healings, prophecies, exorcisms, and miracles in the histories of this movement (cf., Palladius, *The Lausiac History,* Athanasius' *Life of Antony,* the *Historia Monachorum,* the histories of Socrates and Sozomen, etc.)[4] The movement maintained a high degree of vitality for two centuries and culminated, in the west, in the Benedictine movement (of Benedict there are again miracles and prophecies recorded) and in the east in numerous monasteries.

Perhaps the most outstanding prophet of this period was John of Lycopolis. His prophetic powers were attested by Palladius, Sozomen, Augustine, Cassian, and the *Historia Monachorum.*[5] Palladius, for instance, says that John "was deemed worthy of the gift of prophecy. Among other things, he dispatched various predictions to the blessed emperor Theodosius in regard to Maximus the tyrant, that he would conquer him and return from the Gauls." John also prophesied that Palladius' brother had been "converted" and that Palladius himself would become a bishop. All this proved true.[6] Sozomen records that John correctly prophesied the death of Theodosius and Eugenius.[7]

Numerous other ascetics possessed the gift of prophecy, or at least prophesied at one time or another (e.g., Didymus,[8] Marcarius of Egypt,[9] Isidore[10]). The ascetics considered the gift of prophecy to be a great blessing, but not an unexpected one for people who sought to follow God.

A second movement of renewal involving similar charismatic activity swept through the western church in the twelfth and thirteenth centuries. The Cistercian movement, which arose in France during the twelfth century, and the Franciscan and Dominican movements, beginning in Italy at the start of the thirteenth century, wrought a massive change in the church. All three of these movements (which appeared as components of a broader movement in the church of the time) were accompanied by prophecy, healings, miracles and other manifestations of charismatic activity.[11]

Other major and minor movements of renewal in the church could be included in such a review of prophetic activity (e.g., the Hesychasts in the east, and even the American "Second Great Awakening").[12] There have of course been many other incidents of prophecy, either manifest in the life of a particular individual or in groups of people for short periods of time. But, taken as a whole, the history of prophecy in the church since the third century is characterized primarily by movements of renewal which exhibited a wide variety of charismatic activities.

In the twentieth century this phenomenon has been repeated in a "charismatic movement" originating in the United States in the first decade of the century and increasing in size and scope over the last seventy years. At the present time this movement comprises roughly thirteen million people in "Pentecostal" denominations, perhaps two hundred thousand persons in the Orthodox and Protestant churches and upwards of five hundred thousand Roman Catholics.

There are two observations worth making about prophetic activity since the early days of the church. The first is that it mainly resurfaced in the context of a broader revival of charismatic gifts. That is not at all surprising, since Paul treats such gifts as prophecy, healing, and miracles (e.g., 1 Cor. 12) as basically one type of gift. Where charismatic activity is prevalent one should not be surprised to see it take many forms.

The second observation is that prophecy and other charismatic gifts flourish in an atmosphere of expectant faith. That is, they operate mainly where they are *expected* by those who receive them. Healing occurs most often when people believe that healing is possible. Francis of Assisi, John of Lycopolis,

Bernard of Clairvaux all expected that God would speak to them. And he did.

Prophecy has at times come into disrepute through abuse. The theory that prophetic activity disappeared gradually in the third century in reaction to some abuses may be accurate. As a result of various heterodox "prophetic" movements—some of which are with us today—Christians have developed considerable reservation in regard to prophetic activity.[13] While in the early church prophets were held in honor,[14] they have since become more and more subject to suspicion. But if God does bestow the prophetic gift upon the church, then we should be able to receive it. I recently read a statement which summarizes well the attitude we should maintain:

> As soon as we speak of prophets people are immediately worried about false prophets. On the contrary, it seems to me that we should pray for prophecy! The problem now is an absence of prophets. It seems that the Holy Spirit is raising up prophets in our midst. We should be attentive. The community can judge the worth of prophecy after it happens, but let it happen first.[15]

There were false prophets even in the times of the New Testament (e.g., 1 John 4:1), but Christians were taught how to handle them (1 John 4 pass., *Didache* 11:7-12). The presence of false prophets did not prevent Christians from recognizing and receiving those who were genuine. In fact, toward the end of the second century, Irenaeus of Lyons wrote a strong denunciation of Christians who wished to suppress prophecy on the grounds that it could possibly be false:

> Others, again, that they might set at naught the gift of the Holy Spirit, which in the latter times has been, by the good pleasure of the Father, poured out upon the human

race, do not accept that gospel of John in which the Lord promised that he would send the Paraclete; but set aside at once both the gospel and the prophetic spirit. Wretched men indeed, who in order not to allow false prophets set aside the gift of prophecy from the church; acting like those who, on account of such as come in hypocrisy, hold themselves aloof from the communion of the brethren. We must conclude, moreover, that these men cannot admit the Apostle Paul either. For in his epistle to the Corinthians, he speaks expressly of prophetical gifts, and recognizes men and women prophesying in the church. Sinning, therefore, in all these particulars, against the spirit of God, they fall into irremissable sin.[16]

The early church had faith that if God gave gifts to his people, he would also provide them the means to safeguard the exercise of those gifts. Prophecy is reappearing in the church today. We need the confidence that we can both benefit from its power and guard against its abuse.

Notes

1. Justin, *Dialogue With Trypho,* in Ante-Nicene Fathers, Vol. I (New York: The Christian Literature Co., 1890), p. 240 (Chapter LXXII).

2. Irenaeus, *Adversus Haereses,* in Ante-Nicene Fathers, Vol. I (New York: The Christian Literature Co., 1890), p. 532.

3. Othmor Pevlev, ed., *Meliton De Sardes: Sur La Paque et La Paque et Fragments* (Paris: Les Editions du Cerf, 1966), p. 122. English translation in Michael Green, *Evangelism in the Early Church* (London: Hodder & Stoughton, 1970), pp. 201-202.

4. Palladius, *Lausiac History,* trans. Robert T. Meyer, Ancient Christian Writers, no. 34 (Westminster, Md.: Newman Press, 1965); Athanasius. *Life of Antony,* Early Christian Biographies, Fathers of the Church, vol. 15 (New York: Fathers of the Church,

Inc., 1952), pp. 125-216; *Historia Monachorum,* The Paradise of the Fathers, trans. E. Wallis Budge (London: Chatto and Windus, 1907); Socrates, *Ecclesiastical History* and Sozomen, *Ecclesiastical History,* A Select Library of Nicene and Post-Nicene Fathers of the Christian Church, Second Series, vol. II (New York: The Christian Literature Co., 1890).

5. Palladius, *Lausiac History,* pp. 98-103. Sozomen, *Ecclesiastical History,* p. 392. Augustine, *De cura pro mortuis gerenda ad Paulinum episcopum* 17, Corpus Scriptorum Ecclesiasticorum Latinorum 41.655; Cassian, *Conferences* (24.26) and *Institutes* (4.23-26), A Select Library of Nicene and Post-Nicene Fathers of the Christian Church, Second Series, vol. XI (New York: The Christian Literature Co., 1890), pp. 545, 226-227. *Historia Monachorum,* chapter 2.

6. Palladius, *Lausiac History,* ch. 35; Sozomen, *Ecclesiastical History,* VI, 28.

7. Sozomen, *Ecclesiastical History,* VII, 22.

8. Palladius, *Lausiac History,* IV.

9. Palladius, *Lausiac History,* XVII.

10. *Ibid.,* IX, 10.

11. See for instance, on the Cistercians, W.W. Williams, *St. Bernard of Clairvaux* (Manchester: Manchester University Press, 1935), p. 275; on the Franciscans, *The Little Flowers of St. Francis,* trans. Raphael Brown (Garden City, New York: Image/Doubleday, 1958), pp. 96-99, 130-131, 143-147 and Bonaventure, *Major Life of St. Francis,* Chapter 11, St. Francis of Assisi, Omnibus of Sources, ed. Marion Habig (Chicago: Franciscan Herald Press, 1973), pp. 711-720; on the Dominicans, Bede Jarret, *Life of St. Dominic* (Garden City, New York: Image Books, 1924), pp. 87, 118, and Henri Gheon, *St. Vincent Ferrer* (New York: Sheed and Ward, 1954), pp. 108, 115.

12. The history of hesychasm in the Eastern church is not actually that of a clearly defined movement. Rooted as far back as the fourth century ascetic movement, it became a significant spiritual force in the East especially between 1000 and 1453. While certain elements of hesychasm do not lend themselves to extensive prophetic activity, manifestations of prophecy can be found in the lives of different Greek and Russian hesychasts, most notably St. Symeon the New Theologian. See George Maloney, *The Mystic of Fire and Light* (Denville, New Jersey: Dimension Books, 1975), pp. 73, 170-171. For an example from the "Second Great Awakening" see Charles Fin-

ney, *Charles G. Finney: An Autobiography* (Old Tappen, New Jersey: Fleming H Revell Co., 1876) pp. 114-122.

13. E.g., Karl Rahner, *Visions and Prophecies*. Rahner is rather skeptical of visions and revelations—and produces good evidence of the reasonableness of his position. I think that, though Rahner recognizes the distinction between "mystical revelations" and charismatic prophecy, he does not really treat charismatic prophecy in his book. His criteria for discernment do not apply to gifts of prophecy. The book does give a good picture of the grounds for distrust of some revelations, however.

14. Cf., Eph. 2:20, *Didache* 10:7, 13:1, etc.

15. Joseph Hogan, "Charisms of the Holy Spirit," *Restoration,* March 1972, p. 8.

16. *Adversus Haereses,* III, 11, 9.

Chapter Two

What is a Prophet?

Few people today have an accurate or adequate notion of what a Christian prophet is. This is only to be expected: most of us have never met a prophet. In the absence of actual experience our imaginations have taken over. I once wrote an article on prophecy for a magazine, and the illustration which accompanied the article captured perfectly one of the most common conceptions of a prophet: on a rugged and desolate crag of a mountain knelt a bearded and bald old man, his feet unshod and his gaunt body draped with an animal skin. As he gazed intently heavenward, rays of eerie light streamed down from a hidden source to light up his face. If that is a prophet, it's no wonder there are so few!

In order to form a better understanding of Christian prophecy, I want to outline briefly some of the inaccurate or inadequate ideas which float around these days, and compare them with the picture presented to us by Scripture.

One of the most popular understandings of prophecy features the "ecstatic" prophet who whirls around in a sort of a fit or sits in a trance-like state uttering oracles. That is not Christian prophecy. Paul says specifically that "The spirits of the prophets are under the prophets' control, since God is a God, not of confusion, but of peace" (1 Cor. 14:32-33). In a similar way Eusebius of Caesarea, a fourth century Christian historian, contrasts Christian prophets (who are not "ecstatic") and the prophets of a sect called 'Montanism'. Eusebius quotes an earlier Christian writer named Miltiades who had lived in the second century and opposed the Montanists:

> Their (the Montanists') opposition and their recent schismatic heresy in relation to the church originated thus. There is, it appears, a village near the Phrygian border of Mysia called Arbadu. There it is said that a recent convert named Montanus, while Gratus was proconsul in Syria, in his unbridled ambition to reach the top laid himself open to the adversary, was filled with spiritual excitement and suddenly fell into a kind of trance and unnatural ecstasy. He raved, and began to chatter and talk nonsense, prophesying in a way that conflicted with the practice handed down generation by generation from the beginning. . . .[1]

> But the pseudo-prophet speaks in a state of unnatural ecstasy, after which all restraint is thrown to the winds. He begins with voluntary ignorance and ends with involuntary psychosis, as stated already. But they cannot point to a single one of the prophets under either the Old Covenant or the New who was moved by the Spirit in this way— not Agabus or Judas or Silas or Phillip's daughters; not Ammia at Philadelphia or Quadratus; nor any others they may choose to boast about though they are not of their number. . . .[2]

In other words, the Montanists claimed to have the gift of prophecy, but their ecstatic prophets were not behaving like Christian prophets. All the authorities of the early church, from the apostle Paul onward, clearly state that prophets among the Christians have full control of themselves, and do not prophesy in trances and ecstasies.[3]

Another very common notion regarding prophets might be termed "the prophet as a great moral leader." Many Christians derive this view from the great prophets of the Old Testament, who are said to have acted as the "conscience of Israel." Accordingly, they call anyone who exerts striking moral leadership a prophet. Martin Luther King Jr., Mahatma Ghandi and others have been called "prophets." There is some justification for speaking of prophets in this way; the prophets did provide Israel with strong moral leadership. But moral sensitivity and moral leadership do not adequately describe the action of the Holy Spirit in prophecy.

The prophets in the Old Testament brought with them more than an analysis of Israel's moral state—they brought a message from God. They did not claim to speak from their own insight into the affairs of men; they spoke of a judgment given directly by God.[4]

A notion of prophecy very much like that of the "great moral leader" is the notion of the prophet as a "visionary," a man who can "see into things" in a way which normal men cannot. This, too, is inadequate. The prophets of the Old Testament never claimed any special insight *except what was revealed to them by God.*[5] Their ability to understand the things happening around them and to speak of the true meaning underlying those events was not a product of their own "vision"; God was giving them his understanding and vision.

Finally, we have an understanding of prophecy that has become very popular today—the prophet as one who predicts future events. Jeane Dixon, for example, claims the gift of prophecy on the basis of some successful forecasts of the future. Prediction clearly occurs in true prophecy, but it is only a part of the gift. When Paul lists some of the purpose of prophecy, he mentions encouragement, consolation, and the building up of God's people (1 Cor. 14), but not prediction.

We will quickly run into difficulties if we make successful prediction of the future our only criterion for true prophecy. Some people who are not Christian at all can predict future events successfully, yet we cannot accept their "prophecies" as God's word to us. Israel was once sternly warned against those who predicted the future but did not follow the Lord:

> If a prophet arises among you, or a dreamer of dreams, and gives you a sign or a wonder, and the sign or the wonder which he tells you comes to pass, and if he says, "Let us go after other gods," which you have not known, "and let us serve them," you shall not listen to the words of that prophet or to that dreamer of dreams; for the Lord your God is testing you, to know whether you love the Lord your God with all your heart and all your soul. You shall walk after the Lord your God and fear him, and keep his commandments and obey his voice, and you shall serve him and cleave to him. But that prophet or that dreamer of dreams shall be put to death, because he has taught rebellion against the Lord your God. . . .
>
> (Deut. 13:1-5)

In other words, a person can accurately predict future events, yet still be a false prophet.

Well, if all these ways of describing a prophet are inadequate or misleading where can we find an accurate description? I think that the clearest explanation of a true prophet can be found in the book of Exodus as part of a conversation between God and Moses. When God called Moses to take the people of Israel out of Egypt, Moses tried to decline, telling the Lord that he could not speak well enough to talk to the Pharaoh. That excuse didn't help Moses much, however, because God had a solution for the difficulty: Moses' brother Aaron would do the talking:

When he (Aaron) sees you his heart will be glad. You are
to speak with him then, and put the words in his mouth. I
will assist both you and him in speaking and will teach the
two of you what you are to do. He shall speak to the
people for you: he shall be your spokesman, and you shall
be as God to him.

(Exod. 4:15-17)

In that last line, God makes a direct comparison between
the role which Aaron has as Moses' spokesman and the role
which a prophet has as God's spokesman. The common term
for a prophet in Hebrew, "nabi," probably meant "one made to
speak." The standard Greek word, "prophetes," meant "an
interpreter" or "one who speaks for another." Farther on in
the story the Lord says to Moses:

See! I have made you as God to Pharaoh, and Aaron your
brother shall act as your prophet. You shall tell him what I
command you. In turn, your brother Aaron shall tell
Pharaoh to let the Israelites leave his land.

(Exod. 7:1)

That is the role of the prophet—to be a spokesman for God.
A prophet is not a prophet because of what he says, but because of his relationship to God. He is not important in himself, he is important because he comes as a messenger of the
Lord:

And Haggai, the Lord's messenger, proclaimed to the
people as the message of the Lord: I am with you, says the
Lord.

(Hag. 1:13)

To whomever I send you, you shall go; whatever I command you, you shall speak.

(Jer. 1:7)

Then I heard the voice of the Lord saying, "Whom shall I send? Who will go for us?" "Here I am," I said; "send me!" And he replied: "Go and say to this people . . ."
(Isa. 6:8-9)

Son of man, I am sending you to the Israelites . . . But you shall say to them: Thus says the Lord God! . . . Son of man, take into your heart all my words that I speak to you; hear them well. Now go to the exiles, your countrymen, and say to them: Thus says the Lord God!
(Ezek. 2:3-4; 3:10-11)

I was no prophet, nor have I belonged to the company of the prophets; I was a shepherd and a dresser of sycamore trees. The Lord took me from following the flock, and said to me, "Go, prophesy to my people Israel."
(Amos 1:14-15)

In each of these cases God takes a man and makes him a messenger, a spokesman for God himself. The relationship between God and a man is the heart of prophecy.

The Importance of Christian Prophecy

The New Testament prophets were less prominent among the people of God than their predecessors in Israel, though as we have seen, the New Testament prophets still played a vital role. The difference in the role of the prophets under the old and the new dispensations is the result of a change not in the relationship between God and the prophet, but in the relationship between God and his people as a whole. The Old Testament prophet was a man unique among God's people because of the Holy Spirit's action in him. He was in direct communication with the Lord, while the people as a whole were not. But under the New Covenant, *all* of God's people receive the

Holy Spirit, all *all* of God's people are in direct communication with God himself. In Old Testament Israel the prophet was thoroughly unique; in the "new Israel" the prophet is one means among many by which God can speak directly to his people.

But the relationship of God to the prophet, the relationship of king to messenger, remains the same in the New Testament. All of God's people can now hear God's word directly without the mediation of the prophet, yet the prophet remains an official spokesman, authorized to publicly declare the word of God. The image of God as a king ruling his people can illustrate the role of the prophet under both the old and the new dispensations.

Let us imagine God as a king, seated upon the throne in his castle. Under the Old Covenant, the people were greatly blessed by God because (1) God himself was their king; (2) his palace was with them, in the midst of their city; (3) God would from time to time call men into his presence and through them speak to his people. But most of the people could not themselves enter the palace and hear the words of the king from his own mouth.

But under the New Covenant God throws open the gates of the palace and all of his people can themselves enter (Heb. 10:19). Thus, each of God's subjects can hear God's word from his own lips. Under this new arrangement, there still remains a role for the prophet. When a king chooses a messenger from among his people, he provides him with both a message *and with the authority to proclaim the message publicly*. The many subjects who can now enter the palace can hear a message directly from God, but he does not confer upon them the authority to publicly proclaim the message. The prophet then retains a unique function in declaring publicly the word of the Lord. For instance, let us say that the king has a message to declare to all of his subjects in a particular province. Many individual subjects can come into the presence of the king. But he will not speak to all of them about the message he has for that province. Probably he will speak to most of his subjects about matters which refer to them individually. Perhaps he will tell some of them "I am about to send this message to the province." But it would be inappropriate for those subjects to return to the province, mount the royal grandstand and proclaim that the king says "such and such." The king did not ask or authorize those people to act as his official messenger. He entrusts that specific task to his appointed messengers.

Of course it is a mistake to carry such analogies too far. There are important differences between God's dealings with his people and this royal messenger illustration, differences which I will point out later. For the moment, this example can serve to illustrate some aspects of the change from the Old Testament prophets to the New Testament prophets. The prophet in the New Testament is less prominent than the prophet in the Old Testament, but the relationship to God as a divine messenger is preserved, and the prophet retains an important role. The language of the messenger bringing God's word remains "Thus says the Holy Spirit . . ." (Acts 21:11).

Four characteristic functions of Christian prophecy can be used to demonstrate the importance of the gift.

Initiates the Action of God

Prophets frequently initiate the action of God among God's people. Though it is possible for all Christians to hear the voice of the Lord, we very often do not hear God speaking to all of us personally about his will and his plan. Sometimes we fail to hear the Lord because we are not attentive, or because distracting thoughts or personal problems cloud our minds. Very often too God simply elects to speak to us through his prophets. We have no reason to believe that the Lord spoke to anyone but Agabus about the famine which afflicted the Roman empire in the years 49-50. Yet the disciples were stirred to action by this prophetic message and undertook famine relief for Christians in Judea (Acts 11:27ff.). In a very similar way, the Lord spoke through prophecy to a group of Christians in Beirut, Lebanon during the civil war in the fall of 1975, telling them to leave their homes and take refuge temporarily in the United States. Prior to that time, they had all felt they should remain in Beirut despite the fierce fighting which racked the city. Shortly after their departure their section of the city came under heavy attack, and the building they had lived in was bombed.

Awakens God's People to Hear His Word

Prophets can awaken God's people to hear his word. When John prophesied to the church at Sardis that they should "awake and strengthen what remains and is on the point of death," he was trying to shake them from a slumber that was taking their very life. It was not that the Christians at Sardis *could* not have heard that word themselves; they just *did* not hear it. I recall a time two years ago in our community when we seemed to be losing our vitality. We did not very often speak about what the Lord was saying to us or where he was leading us. Then the Lord spoke to us through prophecy: "Repent and restore me to the center of your attention where I ought to be." We seemed to wake up and take notice of our growing apathy. The ability which we all had to hear and respond to God's word was stirred up, and soon we were all once again hearing the Lord and experiencing his action. The prophetic word opened our ears and ignited a desire in our hearts to seek and to find God's will for us.

Proclaims God's Word Publicly

The prophetic word is a public word. It focuses our attention *as a group* on the message which the Lord wants us to hear. If we are to respond to the Lord communally, his word has to be presented to us publicly. Prophecy is not the only way in which the word of the Lord can be made public, but very often prophecy is the means which God will choose to draw our common attention to the word which he wants us to hear.

Unleashes the Power of the Holy Spirit

Through the gift of prophecy the power of the Holy Spirit, at work in the word of God, is unleashed among us. When someone speaks prophetically, the Holy Spirit is at work both in the person who speaks and in all of those who hear. This is a very important truth, and a key to understanding the power of the prophetic word: when God speaks things happen. "By the word of the Lord the heavens were made, and all of their host by the breath of his mouth" (Ps. 33:6).

God's word is a word of power and authority. When the Lord, in the vision of Ezekiel, made the valley of dry bones a living army, he did it through the word which Ezekiel spoke. A very real spiritual power abides in the prophetic word, a power that can change people. It can change the course of nature and of history: "Behold, I make my words in your mouth a fire, and this people is the wood that it shall devour!" (Jer. 5:14).

The speaking of the prophetic word itself brings into action the power of God.[6] Four years ago during a meeting of our community one of the leaders stood up and said "I believe that the Lord has shown me that there is a man present here who is living in sin." He went on to describe the circumstances of the man's life, and told him that he could, right at that moment, turn to God and receive forgiveness and the power to change. At the end of the meeting a young man rose and told us all that he was the individual the Lord had spoken to. He changed his life and became a Christian at that moment. He had heard of Christianity many times before, but when the word of the Lord came directly to him, he experienced an immediate change of heart and a desire to live as a Christian. The prophetic word changed him.

The Purposes of Prophecy

God sends his word for a purpose, to accomplish something in the world:

> For just as from the heavens
> > the rain and the snow come down
> And do not return there
> > till they have watered the earth,
> > making it fertile and fruitful,
> Giving seed to him who sows
> > and bread to him who eats,
> So shall my word be
> > that goes forth from my mouth;
> It shall not return to me void,
> > but shall do my will,
> > achieving the end for which I sent it.

(Isa. 55:10-11)

There are four distinct purposes for which God gives the prophetic gift to the church.

Encouragement

Most often God's word through prophecy is a message of encouragement or exhortation. Paul lists encouragement as one of the benefits of prophecy (1 Cor. 14:3), and Acts 15:32 records the prophets Judas and Silas "encouraging and strengthening" the believers at Antioch.

Encouragement, in the New Testament sense, is intended to revive a person's spirits, to strengthen him or give him hope. All of God's people at times run into difficulty or opposition, and at those times need to hear that God is with them, that he will help them, that he loves them. An excellent example of prophecy sent by God to encourage can be found in the book of Haggai. The Jews returning from exile to Jerusalem had begun to rebuild the city and its temple, but pressure from surrounding enemies had soon caused them to cease. Eighteen years later the Lord's words of encouragement through his messenger Haggai fired them to return to the work:

> Haggai, the messenger of Yahweh, passed on the message of Yahweh to the people, as follows, "I am with you—it is Yahweh who speaks." And Yahweh roused the spirit of Zerubbabel son of Shealtiel, high commissioner of Judah, the spirit of Joshua son of Jehozadak, the high priest, and the spirit of all the remnant of the people; and they came and set to work on the temple of Yahweh Sabaoth their God.
>
> (Hag. 1:13-15)

Many of the prophetic messages which we hear are as simple and unspectacular as the message which God addressed to the Israelites through Haggai: "I am with you, says the Lord." And yet a simple word like that, received with faith, can be profoundly encouraging. It is only a simple expression of concern and support, but the speaker is God.

Conviction, Admonition, Correction

The Holy Spirit will reveal to us our sin, so that we can turn away from sin and be freed from its tyranny. In this aspect of his work, the Holy Spirit can be likened to the defense attorney in a trial. There are, in most legal proceedings, two people who will point out to the defendant his wrongdoing. The prosecuting attorney will expose the defendant's wrongdoing in order to secure his punishment. The defense attorney, on the other hand, will also point out to the defendant where he has done wrong, not in order to condemn him, but in order to save him. Satan, "the accuser," corresponds in this analogy to the attorney for the prosecution; his goal is our condemnation. But the Holy Spirit, like the attorney for the defense, reveals our sin so that we might escape condemnation.

In Isaiah, the Lord says, "a voice shall sound in your ears: 'This is the way, walk in it,' when you turn to the right or the left" (30:21). In other words, God will let us know when we do wrong, and will warn us when we are about to do wrong, so that we can escape from the deception and the power of sin. Through the gift of prophecy that voice sounds in our ears: ". . . put away from yourselves your anger, your jealousy, your irritability. . . ." "Turn your hearts back to me. . . ."

Prophetic admonition or correction can be directed to either groups or individuals. Several months ago a young married couple, who had not been Christians, began to come to our community meetings. They were seeking God, but were not convinced that he could be found in Christianity. They were also being troubled by jealousy and animosity in their own relationship. During one of the first meetings they attended, the husband was feeling great doubt that Christianity held out any hope for him at all. He silently offered an almost despairing prayer, asking for some sign that God could be found among Christians. At the very moment he concluded that prayer, another young man stood to speak: "I believe that God has shown me a young married couple present at this meeting tonight" (there were about six hundred people at the meeting). "These people are seeking God, but are encountering doubt and confusion. Furthermore, they are having difficulty in their own relationship because of anger and jealousy." He went on to tell them, in the name of the Lord, that if they forgave one another and trusted in God, God would reveal himself to them and strengthen their marriage. Of course, the young husband was thunderstruck. This person had perfectly described their situation, and offered a solution at the very moment he had asked for it. The young man who spoke to them in prophecy had neither met them nor ever heard of them. That young couple heeded God's word, repented of their anger with one another, and are now living happily as Christians.

Inspiration

Very often prophecy will function in the church as a source of inspiration. When the gift functions in this way, the Holy Spirit is primarily *doing* something to people through prophecy rather than *saying* something to them. Of course, since prophecy is a gift operating through speech, something will always be said. But inspirational prophecy is not so much concerned with communicating information as with evoking a response.

Frequently people have commented to me that they are troubled because they do not always remember what has been said in prophecy at a community meeting. That is a problem only when the Lord is intent upon giving us direction or telling us something specific. Most of the time, however, the intention of the Holy Spirit is simply to lead the community in a worshipful response to God. At those times, the important thing is to respond to God, not to remember the exact words of the prophecy. Prophecy seemed to occupy a prominent place in the worship of the early church (cf., *Didache* 10). The gift enabled the prophet to lead the people in praise and thanksgiving. I have seen the value of prophecy for worship in our own community and in many others. It brings the Holy Spirit *into* the group in a powerful way. Literally, it *inspires* people.

In 1 Chronicles 25:3 we read of prophets participating in the solemn worship of Yahweh. There is reason to believe that at least some sections of the psalms are prophetic oracles which originated in ritual worship (e.g., Ps. 46:11; 81:6-17). The following prophecy, spoken at a gathering of our community, is an example of a powerful inspirational prophecy, calling people to worship and impelling them to glorify God:

Yes my people, my beloved children,
  come into my presence, be with me today.
Worship me for I am here among you.
Open your hearts to me: let me fill you with my love.
Let me clothe you in my righteousness as you bow before
  me.
I am the Lord your God, the mighty God of all.

Be assured of my love for you.
Be assured that I am with you.
Open now your hearts to me;
  give your lives to me.

Move with me; as I bid you, come.
Know the love of your God.
And know the life of his people.
Indeed, I am with you.

Guidance

All through the Scriptures, we read of God speaking to his people to guide them into his ways. Sometimes his guidance was very general: he revealed his plan for salvation and gave men a way of knowing him and following him in all ages. But at times that guidance was very specific, even to the point of telling Israel what political alliances to make or warning a man that he would die within a year if he did not repent (Jer. 28:16). In the time after Jesus, God spoke through prophecy and warned of a famine (Acts 11:27ff.). Many people also believe that the Lord used prophecy to warn the Christians in Jerusalem about the impending destruction of the city by the Romans, so that before the city was actually destroyed all the Christians moved to the nearby town of Pella. The guidance received by Christians in Beirut which I described earlier is a modern day counterpart to the story of the Christians at Jerusalem.

The guidance which we receive from God can apply to important directional questions as well as to specific individual needs. Peter received prophetic guidance concerning the salvation of the Gentiles (Acts 10:9-16), and Paul states that it was in part through the prophets that he received his gospel for the Gentiles (Eph. 3:5).

The church today needs guidance from God as much as it ever did. The difficulties and questions which confront those who are trying to spread the Gospel are formidable, in fact insurmountable, unless God provides the means to overcome them. The direct guidance of God is available to us when we need it. The gift of prophecy is one of the most important means by which God can guide and direct us, and we should not be without it.

On two occasions at least I have been involved in planning meetings in which prophetic guidance played a decisive role. On the first occasion the group I was working with had no clear sense of direction for its work. We stopped for a few moments and prayed. During those few moments, one person present spoke in prophecy. The words were straightforward direction for our meeting: "Put your own relationships in order first." The "relationships" in question were not simply personal relationships, but work relationships as well. The prophecy was directed at our practical needs. We resumed our discussion and followed out the directive to "put our relationships in order." The results were spectacular. From that discussion flowed a clear, practical direction which has since molded the whole life of our community.

The second occasion on which prophetic guidance was decisive occurred only eight months before I wrote this book. We had a set of goals, but try as we would, we could not discover a way to implement them. We simply had too many tasks to accomplish with too few people. So we turned to God and asked for help. We asked the Lord to show us what each person present should be doing. We received specific guidance for each person, and when the whole thing was put together, all the problems had been solved. God had shown us by revelation what we could not figure out on our own.

Relying on prophecy for guidance can create problems if we expect that every decision we face will be made for us in a prophecy. We could adopt the attitude that we do not have to think about things ourselves, because if we wait long enough the answer will be given prophetically. But the desire to avoid this abuse is no reason to avoid prophecy altogether. The help which we see prophets giving in the Old Testament is still available in the New; when we face an important decision we can ask the prophets if they have a word from the Lord. Old Testament prophets did not "guarantee" that they would receive a word from the Lord if they were asked about something, but they did have expectant faith that if God's people sincerely wished to know his ways, he would not withhold his word from them. Often the Lord will use prophecy to guide us into his ways when we are not expecting it. Sometimes when we do expect prophetic guidance the Lord will not speak prophetically. But if we have faith that God will give us guidance, he will, and much of that guidance will come through prophecy.

All in all, the access to the mind of the Lord which the gift of prophecy provides is a powerful, valuable resource. Valuable enough that we should all, as Paul encourages us "set our hearts on spiritual gifts—above all the gift of prophecy" (1 Cor. 14:1).

Notes

1. Eusebius, *The History of the Church*, trans. G. A. Williamson (Baltimore, Maryland: Penguin, 1965) Book V, 16, pp. 218-219.

2. Eusebius, *The History of the Church*, Book V, 17.

3. Cf., Abraham J. Heschel, *The Prophets*, vol. II (New York: Harper and Row, 1971) chapters 8, 9.

4. Heschel, *The Prophets*, p. 207. Bruce Vawter, "Introduction to Prophetic Literature," *The Jerome Biblical Commentary*, ed. Raymond Brown, Joseph Fitzmeyer, and Roland Murphy (Englewood Cliffs, New Jersey: Prentice-Hall, 1968), pp. 227, 234.

5. Heschel, *The Prophets*, p. 207.

6. Vawter, "Introduction to Prophetic Literature," p. 237.

Chapter Three

The Prophet's Role

The designation of prophets as "messengers" of God has been developed in order to highlight two central aspects of the prophet's mission: the objective and divine nature of the word which he brings, and his divine authorization to proclaim the message to God's people. But to restrict the vision of the prophet to the elements introduced in the designation as "messenger" does an injustice to the very active and diversified task which God sets for him. The prophets clearly saw themselves as God's "messengers" (Isa. 44:26, Hag. 1:13, Mal. 3:1). They also considered themselves "servants of God" (Isa. 20:3, Amos 3:7, Jer. 7:25, 24:4, etc.), "guardians" of Israel (Isa. 62:6), and "watchmen" (Amos 3:4, Isa. 56:10, Jer. 6:17, Ezek. 3:17).

The prophets were, in their own eyes, entrusted with a mission demanding much more than passive receptivity to inspirations that might overtake them. Once a man knew that he had been called to be a prophet, he devoted himself wholeheartedly and very actively to his task. "We may indeed quite properly speak of the prophetic 'office', consisting on the one hand of binding commitments, and on the other of liberties and powers."[1] The prophets used every occasion and circumstance to proclaim the message they had received from God. For the sake of their missions Hosea married a prostitute and Jeremiah refrained from marriage entirely (Hos. 1:2, Jer. 16:2). Amos quit his home and his occupation to fulfill his call (Amos 7:12ff.).

In the New Testament the pattern continued. While many Christians prophesied from time to time, or even regularly for periods of time, some of them were specially equipped to fulfill the role of the prophet:

> According to Acts (2:16ff.) St. Peter interpreted the miracle of Pentecost as evidence that the whole church was a prophetic community, animated by the Holy Spirit. God had fulfilled Joel's oracle, "Your sons and your daughters shall prophesy." But from the New Testament as a whole it is clear that certain individuals were specially called to exercise the prophetic ministry (Rom. 12:6, 1 Cor. 12:6-10, 28-29.)[2]

Not all of those who prophesy are prophets. Paul says in 1 Corinthians 14 that all can prophesy (v. 31), but he also asks "Are all prophets?" and the answer is "no." Paul speaks both of "spirituals" and of "gifts of the spirit" and the two are not the same. A "spiritual" is a manifestation—a breaking forth—of the power of the Holy Spirit in prophecy (or in healing, working a miracle, etc.). A "gift of the Holy Spirit" is the equipment which fits an individual to take his particular role among God's people. In other words, Paul says that many can prophesy by a "working of the Holy Spirit," but that only some have the "gift" to be a prophet. (See appendix 2).

An Old Testament prophet knew that when the Israelites needed to hear God's word, he could quite appropriately go before Yahweh and ask for it. That was his place, his role as a prophet. He knew furthermore that his task in delivering God's word was not completed when he first proclaimed the "message" God had given him. He preached it when the occasion provided the opportunity. Jeremiah committed his prophecy to writing at God's command so that it could be presented to the king (Jer. 36). Ezekiel was quite clearly told by God that his task included not merely the reception and subsequent pronouncement of a word, but also active and ongoing vigilance in speaking that word when occasion demanded it (Ezek. 3).

The Prophet's Role

A true Christian prophet has a role demanding the same vigilance and the same sustained exercise of responsibility. His role can be described under five headings: to receive and proclaim the word; to actively seek out God's will and God's word; to "stir up" his gift; to "watch over" the word given and see it acted upon and fulfilled; and to intercede before God on behalf of the church.

Receiving and Proclaiming the "Word"

A more apt description of this responsibility would perhaps be "obeying the promptings of the Spirit." A crucial part of the prophetic ministry is immediate and obedient response to the urging of the Holy Spirit, whether that be a prompting to speak a message, perform a prophetic action, or even to refrain from speaking for a time. Yahweh said to Ezekiel "Whenever you hear a word from me, warn them in my name" (Ezek. 3:17). When the Lord told Jeremiah to go visit the house of the potter, Jeremiah went (Jer. 18). When the Lord told Isaiah that King Hezekiah would recover from an illness, Isaiah immediately went to the king with that message, even though he had prophesied only moments before that the king would *not* recover (2 Kings 20). When Agabus heard the Spirit telling him to bind the hands of Paul and prophesy, he did so at once (Acts 21:11).

Of what use is a servant who will not do his master's will? What good is a messenger who does not proclaim the message he is given? Paul would most certainly have been to blame had he not responded to the dream calling him to Macedonia (Acts 16:9). The same blame should fall to the prophet who hears a word from the Lord and fails to speak it.

Actively Seeking Out God's Will and God's Word

The prophet bears a responsibility to place himself continually in the presence of God, seeking to hear the word of the Lord and asking the Lord for guidance and direction, for encouragement or rebuke. When the Christian community needs guidance, it can rightly look to its prophets for a word from the Lord. When the community gathers to worship, it can rightly look to its prophets for inspired prayer or song, or words of improvement, encouragement or consolation (1 Cor. 14:3).

I have witnessed occasions when God *has* granted a prophetic word in response to people who sought it and occasions when he has not. I have already described two meetings in which God, through prophecy, gave very practical solutions for difficulties (see p. 44). Before those two meetings, we were not particularly confident that God would speak to us directly on what were, after all, simple practical matters. Yet we received important prophetic revelation when we asked for it. As I write this book, some members of our community are trying to solve a very difficult problem involving a shortage of office space. They have asked the Lord to reveal what they should do. But, at this point at least, the Lord has not given them any prophetic guidance.

It is entirely appropriate for prophets to seek God for his word on any and every occasion. Perhaps God will speak, perhaps he will not. But it is the duty of the messenger to be in his presence, ready and eager to convey any word he may wish to send.

"Stirring Up" the Prophetic Gift

Paul tells us in 1 Corinthians that "prophets can always control their prophetic spirits" or as another translation puts it, "the spirits of prophets are subject to prophets" (14:32). Paul means primarily that prophets can *refrain* from prophesying when that is appropriate. But I believe that there is also a positive aspect to the control which prophets can exercise over their gift.

When God assigns someone a responsibility in the Christian community, he also provides him with the necessary gifts. God will not indicate that he has given an individual a mission of evangelism unless he also has given that person the gift to evangelize. And because the individual can count upon God's power in his assigned service, he can make *initiatives* in that service. For instance, a person who knows that God has called him to an evangelistic service can place himself in situations where he will have to evangelize. It would be appropriate for him, as it was for Paul in Athens or in Corinth, to assemble people for the express purpose of preaching the good news to them. He could then expect that God would supply the spiritual power necessary to open people's hearts to the gospel.

The same basic truth applies to prophetic service. If God entrusts an indiviudal with the task of serving the church as a prophet, that individual can count on God's action when he attempts to serve prophetically. It is right, therefore, for a prophet to take initiative in prophecy. No man can prophesy unless the Holy Spirit works in him, but a prophet *can* "arouse" or "stir up" or "call into action" the gift that has been given to him. When Paul addresses Timothy, he urges him to "stir up" the gift he has been given (2 Tim. 1:6).

Spiritual gifts can be viewed as tools which God provides to help "build up the body of Christ" (cf., Eph. 4:7-16). Those who are given these tools are entrusted with carrying out the corresponding tasks, just as a carpenter, for instance, is entrusted with the task for which his tools and his training suit him. The architect does not tell the carpenter every blow to strike with his hammer. Instead, he gives the carpenter blueprints and trusts him to make something according to those blueprints. This does not mean that a prophet can prophesy whatever he wishes and whenever he wishes. Prophecy will *always* depend upon the action of the Holy Spirit. But it does mean that a prophet can bring the power of the Holy Spirit into action. He can make the prophetic gift active when the occasion calls for it.

The prophet, in other words, can prophesy whenever it is appropriate, so long as he has a word from the Lord. Jeremiah did not have to wait passively for a moment of inspiration to strike him. He knew the Lord's word for Israel, and he could bring the power of his prophetic gift into action simply by speaking that word. The importance of this ability to "prophesy" at the initiative and discretion of the prophet depends upon an understanding of the power of the prophetic word itself. Prophecy is more than simple communication of a message. It involves an action of the Holy Spirit, an unleashing of the power of the Holy Spirit (see p. 38). That spiritual power is a significant part of the prophet's gift. Any Christian who knows the Lord's word for a particular time and place can repeat that word. But a prophet can *prophesy* that word. He can declare it with full authority, and he can expect God to work through his declaration.

"Watching Over" the Prophetic Word

The Lord told Ezekiel, Jeremiah, Isaiah, and the other prophets of Israel that their responsibility went beyond the first time they spoke the word he gave them; they were to continue speaking that word until Israel either responded to it or finally rejected it. So too, a person given the role of the prophet in the church has to repeat and insist upon the word which he has been given until God's people hear it and respond to it.

Praying for the Church

I believe that an integral and important part of the prophet's task is unceasing prayer for the Christian community. The prophets, because they knew what the mind of the Lord was, were in a position to pray more effectually than other men. They had a clearer picture of what God was doing, and so they knew when prayer was most needed. They were also able to pray true "prophetic prayers," in which the Holy Spirit directed and guided their very manner and words. "Upon your walls, Jerusalem, I set watchmen. *Day or night they must never be silent. You who keep Yahweh mindful must take no rest. Nor let him take rest till he has restored Jerusalem*" (Isa. 62:6, italics mine).

The prophet, then, is not a man who simply leaves himself open to the possible inspiration of the Spirit. Rather, he is entrusted with a task demanding responsibility and vigilance on his part. He is to make himself active in the role which God has assigned him.

Identifying a Prohetic Gift

The Old Testament prophets knew they were prophets because they had experienced a definite and life-shaping encounter with God, an encounter in which God clearly gave them a prophetic assignment. That encounter made them prophets. The New Testament contains no accounts of prophetic "calls." Undoubtedly there were some such calls from God; we know at least that Paul began his ministry as an apostle in response to such a call (Acts 13:1ff., Gal. 1:11ff.). And we know that Timothy learned from a prophetic message that a particular spiritual gift had been given to him (1 Tim. 4:14). It is reasonable to suppose that some Christian prophets do experience a direct "calling" to a prophetic service.

But whether a person receives a direct call or not, the burden for determining who is to function as a prophet within the Christian community falls to the elders, not to the prophets (see below, chapter 5). It is necessary therefore to know how a true prophet can be identified. There are two categories of qualifications for the exercise of a prophetic ministry: the personal life of the prophet, and the manifestation of the spiritual gift of prophecy.

The Life of the Prophet

No one can effectively serve God in a position of real responsibility unless his life is solid and stable, in both its Christian and its normal human aspects. A person afflicted with emotional or psychological problems cannot be trusted with a place of responsibility and authority within the community. God offers healing and strength to those who need it, but they should receive that healing before they are allowed to function in a prophetic service (or any other responsible service). Furthermore, any person not living a strong and consistent Christian life should not be allowed to function as a leader of God's people.

We will from time to time encounter individuals who seem to manifest impressive spiritual gifts, and try to claim a place of service in the community on the basis of their powers. Frequently their spiritual powers are genuine. But it is not spiritual powers alone that determine positions of service in the body of Christ. Some time ago our community encountered an individual who seemed to "prophesy" with real power. His prophetic gift was, I believe, genuine. However, this individual also manifested significant emotional immaturity in his personal life. As a consequence, the community could not fully trust this person's exercise of prophetic gifts.

Since he could not be unqualifiedly trusted, it was better that he refrain from prophesying until he had attained the requisite emotional stability.

Manifestation of Spiritual Gifts

Many individuals in the community will experience "manifestations" of prophecy, but the simple fact of prophesying does not indicate that an individual is a prophet. Before crediting someone with a significant gift of prophecy, we must see in him a more powerful, consistent and complex manifestation of the prophetic spirit. There are four primary characteristics of an abiding prophetic gift.

First, *an ongoing and consistent exercise of prophecy.* Most people in the community prophesy only occasionally, or they may prophesy regularly for only a relatively short period of time (perhaps two or three years). Not uncommonly, people who have newly entered the community will prophesy regularly for a while. Only when an individual prophesies regularly over a period of four or five years or longer should we begin considering whether the gift is a significant indication of his place of service.

Secondly, a prophet should manifest *a powerful and effective exercise of prophetic gifts.* True prophecy can be manifested with more or less spiritual power. A significant prophecy has an impact on those who hear it; it is life-changing and life-producing. We should look for "results" from the exercise of an individual's prophetic gifts. If his prophecy consistently changes people, moves the community forward in God's purpose—in short, has appreciable effect on the life of the community—then we can safely assume that God has given him prophetic gifts in important measure.

Third, a prophet should have the *ability to "stir up" the gift.* Prophets can be counted upon to exercise their gifts when the community needs them. They are reliable; and they can be reliable because they have been sufficiently equipped by God to fulfill their role. At times a prophet may even learn what will help him bring his gift into action. Elisha asked a minstrel to play for him when the king of Judah asked him to "get the word of the Lord" (2 Kings 3:9-20). Many prophets have experienced times when songs and hymns which glorify the Lord "bring on" the prophetic spirit. This technique is neither mystical nor merely psychological. Christians have long recognized that their environment affects their ability to turn to the Lord. Oftentimes prayer or song can dispose us to receive the word of the Lord.

When an individual is able to consistently make his gift effective for the life of the community, that is an indication that God has entrusted him with the prophetic service in a significant measure.

Finally, an abiding prophetic gift usually includes a *true gift of revelation which operates consistently.* One clear mark of a true prophet is revelation. Through the prophets God reveals mysteries, brings to light his plan, and makes known things which have been hidden. At times prophetic revelation concerns specific private matters. God revealed King David's sin to Nathan so that the prophet could confront David and bring him to repentance. At other times God uses prophets to reveal some major aspect of his plan for the world. For example, the revelation that the Gentiles could take part in salvation without following the Law of Moses came in part through the prophets of the early church (see Eph. 2:4-6).

Not all revelation shows us something entirely new. But many of the mysteries of the Christian faith will be revealed in greater clarity, with a greater fullness by the prophets. Through the many prophecies I have heard describing God's love, I have come to a much fuller and deeper understanding of that love. This is not simply the effect of repetition. Some of those prophecies opened my eyes to the mystery of the eternal and unfailing love of God. God had already revealed that love to the world, but through the prophets he has revealed it to *me.*

The foregoing characteristics of personal life and spiritual gift can serve as a guide for recognizing the presence of the spiritual gift of prophecy. But they can serve as a guide only—not as an official "checklist." The gifts which Christ assigns to individuals differ. One apostle differs from another in both the degree and character of his gift. Prophets will differ from one another in the same way. I know one person who seems to have a gift only for a kind of "inspirational" prophecy. Yet for some years now he has consistently manifested a powerful and productive inspirational gift. He is also able to "stir up" that gift. His prophetic gift is one of the greatest assets to community worship that I have ever witnessed. To a degree then, it is appropriate to refer to him as "a prophet." He does not receive revelation, but still he is in some sense a true prophet.

Paul tells us that each person should use the gift he has received according to the measure of the gift given to him (Rom. 12:3). Not all prophets are called to prophetic service in the same way or to the same degree. But there is among them a true "family resemblance." In recognizing the likeness between members of the same family we are not surprised to notice individual differences as well: one may have blue eyes and another brown, and so forth. But there remains enough commonality among them all that we can discern their overall resemblance. Prophet may also differ from prophet in the way God uses him in his service.

Recognizing Prophets in the Community

A Christian community must be able to identify those members who have received prophetic gifts. As we shall see in the next chapter, regulation of the prophetic gifts depends heavily upon the community's knowing who the prophets are and how each prophet's gift operates. On the other hand, it is equally important that we not be too eager to label someone a "prophet." Spiritual gifts require time, a lot of time, to reveal themselves in their fullness. At one stage in a Christian's life he may appear to have a prophetic gift; later we may discover that while he does sometimes prophesy, his major gift of service lies more in the area of music (or evangelism, or administration). Making a quick judgment about an area as important as this could lead to trouble. We may end up depending on some individual for a gift he does not have; or we may restrict the full development of his gifts by forcing him to concentrate on what, in God's eyes, is a peripheral element.

Several years ago I watched the way a very wise football coach handled a talented young player. The player had obvious gifts for football; he was big and fast and possessed quick reactions. But throughout the season the coach moved him from one position to another as he learned more about the player's abundant abilities. This necessitated constant change in the coach's whole strategy. But the coach was wise enough to know that his work would be rewarded. He succeeded in producing both a championship team and an All-American football player.

We need to devote the same careful wisdom to the discernment of gifts in the Christian people. We ought not to call someone a prophet before we know that God has called him to an ongoing prophetic service. It is equally unwise to withhold from a real prophet the freedom to grow and develop in his assigned service.

The picture of the prophet which emerges from the pages of Scripture and the early church writings is impressive. Rather than a mere mouthpiece who passively responds when God picks him up, the prophet is a conscious agent of God, gifted by God to be an envoy, a watchman, and a bearer of royal authority.

The prophet, as every other member of the body, is subject to the authority of the community. But in his place of service he exercises a true "charismatic" authority, proclaiming God's word and leading the community in its response to God. In his service to the Lord, the prophet is subject to the community. But in its service to God, the community is subject to the authority of the word which the prophet brings.

Notes

1. Gerhard Von Rad, *Old Testament Theology,* Vol. II, trans. D.M.B. (Stalker, Edinburg: Oliver & Boyd, 1965), p. 38.

2. Avery Dulles, "The Succession of Prophets in the Church," *Apostolic Succession,* ed. Hans Küng, Concilium, vol. 34 (New York: Paulist Press, 1968), p. 53.

Chapter Four

The Government of Prophecy in the Christian Community

If we are to form a clear picture of the operation of prophetic gifts in the church, we must turn back to the period in the church's life when prophecy was an expected daily phenomenon. Unfortunately, the records of the early church do not give us as full and detailed a picture of the activity of prophets as we might have wished. Taken together with contemporary experience, however, they do present us with enough evidence that we can understand in broad outline how the early Christian supervised prophetic activity.

The Need for Discernment

The early Christian church was characterized by an active expectation of God's immediate and visible intervention. The first Christians knew their God to be a God of power not by hearsay or second-hand report, but by direct experience. Some of them had actually seen the resurrected Jesus. They had seen the healing of the man by the "Beautiful Gate" (Acts 3:1-10), the blinding of Elymas the magician (Acts 13:8-12), and the healing of the cripple at Lystra (Acts 14:8-10) testify directly and powerfully to the truth of the gospel. These Christians lived their lives in an atmosphere of expectant faith which many Christians today would find foreign, even uncomfortable.

That very faith is a key to the miracles, healings and prophecy which they experienced. The writer of the letter to the Hebrews says simply, "Now it is impossible to please God without faith, since anyone who comes to him must believe that he exists and rewards those who seek him" (Heb. 11:6). We might say in the same way, "It is impossible to receive prophecy unless you believe that God will speak to you and ask him to do so." The basic claims of prophecy leave us uneasy if we lack faith that God will speak directly to us. Prophets claim that the word they speak is *God's* word and not their own.

The early Christians clearly believed in the divinely inspired authority of prophetic utterance. The prophets themselves employed unequivocal terms in announcing their message: "Thus says the Holy Spirit" (Acts 21:11). And their claim was accepted. The writer of Acts states simply that when Barnabas and Saul were set apart for missionary work it was the Holy Spirit who spoke (Acts 13:2). The early Christian manual, the *Didache,* severely warns Christians not to speak against a prophet who speaks in the Spirit, citing the passage concerning the sin against the Holy Spirit (*Didache* 11:7).[1]

Belief in the divine nature of prophecy is the key to both its value and its dangers. The church covets a gift which brings it the direct word of God (1 Cor. 14:1). At the same time, the exercise of that gift must be carefully safeguarded. There is a danger in acknowledging that men can be directly inspired by God and can speak his word authoritatively. A person could use that claim to invest his own ideas or wishes with the authority of God. Serious damage could obviously befall the church if people were prophesying falsely. And of course, damage has come to the church through just such abuses.

To shun prophecy because of its inherent dangers is no solution, however. In some way, the church must keep the benefits of true prophecy while avoiding the dangers of false prophecy. Paul advises the Christians at Thessalonica, "Do not despise prophesying, but test everything; hold fast that which is good" (1 Thess. 5:20-21). John repeats the advice: "Beloved, do not believe every spirit, but test the spirits to see whether they are of God; for many false prophets have gone out into the world" (1 John 4:1). The *Didache* recommends various measures to separate true prophets from the false *(Didache* 11:3f.) The early church must then have had some means for deciding what was true and what was false.

In order to examine the methods for discernment adopted by the first century Christians, we must consider two important elements of Christian life, elements upon which the ability to make right judgments about prophecy rested.

First of all, the early Christians lived a highly communal life. True, the picture presented in Acts (2:42-47, 4:32-37) probably did not represent the experience of all Christian communities. But it is clear from the New Testament that Christians did live a life which kept them in daily contact with one another, and in which they knew one another quite well.[2] Their gospel of "love for the brothers" in a new nation, separate from the world around them and ruled over by the risen Lord Jesus, demanded mutual personal concern. The rapid expansion of Christianity after Constantine and the various social transformations of the succeeding centuries perhaps obliterated community life as it was known to those at Corinth, Rome or Philippi. But for them, the gospel meant living the life of the kingdom here and now, loving one another as Christ loved us.

Furthermore, as citizens of the heavenly kingdom, they shared with one another their deepest concerns. They were not concerned with the same things as other men. God could speak to them all, and at one time touch the desires which motivated all of their lives. That unity of heart and mind and will (cf., Phil. 2:1ff.) meant that, Jew or Greek, slave or free, God could speak to them all with one word.

The second basic element of early Christian life which affected the discernment of prophecy was the position of elders. Each community was governed by a group of elders who taught, led the community in worship, governed its common life and worked out disputes. The elders, in addition, bore a special responsibility for protecting the community against false prophets and teachers (cf., Acts 20:28-31, Titus 1:10-16, 2 Tim. 4:1-5, 1 Thess. 5:14). These men carried the authority to credit or discredit prophets and prophetic utterance.[3]

The Process of Discernment

When we examine the statements of the New Testament and the early church manuals in regard to discerning prophecy, we are first of all struck by the fact that they are almost exclusively concerned with discerning (i.e., passing judgment upon) *prophets* rather than *prophecies*. The warnings of the Epistles are directed toward false prophets, not toward specific false prophecies. Similarly, the *Didache* gives rules for determining whether a prophet is true or false, not whether his prophecies are true or false (11:5,6,12). Why the focus on the person rather than the prophecy?

First, most prophecies do not require any significant direct response. The majority of prophecies serve purposes of encouragement and exhortation. They do not of themselves demand any decision as to whether or not they are directly inspired. For instance, there would be no real need to determine whether the prophecy given by bishop Melito (quoted on pp. 21-22) was, in fact, directly inspired. The import of the prophecy is true and faithbuilding, whether or not it was directly inspired. The great majority of prophecies given in Christian communities are of this kind.

Secondly, a community rarely has to depend upon a single inspired utterance in order to determine major directional questions. At times the prophetic word *will* demand a definite response—when the Holy Spirit spoke to the elders in Antioch about sending out Saul and Barnabas (Acts 13:1), they had to know whether the utterance was truly from God. Their decision to send the two men out on a mission was tantamount to declaring that the utterance truly represented God's will. On the other hand, a decision to keep Barnabas and Saul in Antioch would have amounted to saying that they did not believe the utterance was inspired. Some definitive response had to be made. But I greatly doubt that their decision was based upon that single utterance taken in isolation.

Most often, when definite responses to prophecy are required, The Lord will speak to several people in the community and not just to a single prophet. I think we can safely imagine that the elders at Antioch had some evidence that God wanted Saul and Barnabas sent out before the particular statement recorded in Acts was ever spoken. My own experience, and the experience of many others today, would indicate that significant decisions rarely proceed on the strength of an isolated prophetic statement. Rather, the spirit which is common to the prophets and to the whole community as well provides us with ample testimony to the inspiration of the prophecies which do come.

Finally, most of the early literature is concerned with testing prophets and not prophecies simply because testing prophets, and then trusting to the gifts of the accredited prophets, was the main method by which prophecy was judged. The early Christians could trust the word of a prophet because they knew him to be a prophet. The fact that a person was known to be a true prophet in itself constituted significant evidence that any prophecy he spoke was divinely inspired.

Some rather minimal tests of *prophecies* are supplied in the New Testament. Paul tells us in 1 Corinthians 12:3 that no one speaking under the influence of the Holy Spirit can say "Curse Jesus." But beyond such basic tests neither the New Testament nor any other early Christian document supplies any means for testing specific prophetic statements. Once it is determined that the speaker is neither possessed by an evil spirit nor an outright heretic, you cannot go much further in judging his prophecy.

Our question then must be, how did the church recognize the true prophets, the prophets upon whom it could rely for revelation? The answer has for the most part been given in a preceding chapter: first examine the life of the individual, then examine the effects of his or her prophecy on the community. These criteria can be elaborated.

The Life of the Prophet

As stated earlier, the prophet must first of all be living a solid and stable Christian life. He must be emotionally mature and sound in judgment. He must be, in the scriptural sense of the term, a "spiritual" person.

In the third chapter of the first letter to the Corinthians, Paul tells his hearers that they are not *spiritual* men, but men of the flesh—in spite of the fact that the Corinthians "do not lack any spiritual gift" (1 Cor. 1:7). Jealousy, strife, and division exist among them—evidence of the fallen nature of man rather than of the Holy Spirit of God. In the fifth chapter of Galatians, Paul again sets forth criteria for distinguishing between the spiritual and the unspiritual. If you are led by the Spirit of God, he says, your life will be characterized by love, joy, peace, patience, kindness, goodness, faithfulness, gentleness, and self-control. But if you are unspiritual, your life will be characterized by immorality, indecency, sexual irresponsibility, idolatry, sorcery, feuds, wrangling, jealousy, bad temper, disagreements, factions, envy and so on. In Ephesians 5:9 he summarizes this approach simply by saying " . . . for the effects of light are seen in complete goodness and right living and truth."

The first letter of John is a study in discernment. The true follower of Christ can be recognized by the way he lives. Does he keep the commandments? Does he love "the brothers"? Does he acknowledge Jesus as the Christ who has come in the flesh? (1 John 2:3, 3:8, 2:9-10, 3:11, 2:23, 4:2-3). In other words, the true follower of Christ, the truly spiritual man, can be known by the fact that he lives according to the Spirit of God and not according to the spirit of darkness or the evil inclinations of his nature.

Implicit in the criterion of prophets is the assumption that members of a community will know one another. The normal community life of the early Christians allowed ample opportunity to observe whether a particular person was or was not "spiritual." The early church also knew of travelling prophets, who moved from community to community, often in groups, as did the apostles. But even then the character of the travelling prophet's life was the fundamental determinant in whether his prophecy was trusted. The *Didache* offers some rules for testing travelling prophets which are summed up in the statement: "It is by their conduct that the false prophet and the (true) prophet can be distinguished" (11:8). Frequently, the head of a local community would have visiting prophets stay in his home, thus affording a greater opportunity to observe the prophet's conduct. The same method of discernment is described in *The Shepherd of Hermas* (Mand. 11).[4]

The Fruit of His Service

If a person is a true prophet of God, then the community will be able to experience the power of the Holy Spirit at work in the words he speaks and will benefit significantly from the effects of heeding his words. At times the prophet will foretell events of one kind or another; the fulfillment of those predictions provides another means to test the efficacy of his service. Or again, he may indicate prophetically that the community should take one direction or another, and the fruit of the community's response will bear witness to the truth of his words.

The community can experience the power at work in prophecy. Spiritual power is not the power of eloquence or simple human sincerity; it is a power that comes through the Holy Spirit. The words of God have life in them. Many times I have witnessed prophets speaking words of refreshment and consolation. When those words proceeded from God, they *effected* refreshment in the people who heard them. Similarly, true prophetic reproof or correction brings with it a greater understanding of and sorrow for sin. If the prophet is inspired when he speaks, his words will produce more than simple human reasoning or eloquence can produce.

When a prophet foretells that certain events will happen, we can watch for the fulfillment of his prophecy. Eight years ago, one member of our community prophesied that many thousands of people would come to our town from all over the world because of the community. At the time, the "community" consisted of a handful of inexperienced college students and recent graduates. We had no reason to expect the events which that prophecy foretold. Yet today, only eight years later, the prophecy has been more than fulfilled. Literally thousands have come to visit the community (over fifteen hundred visitors annually), and they have included leaders of several denominations and people from dozens of nations.

The efficacy of decisions made on the basis of prophetic revelation will also prove whether the prophecy was inspired.

Isaiah told Hezekiah not to surrender to Sennecharib (2 Kings 19), and the later results of that counsel indicated that God had spoken through him.

It would be a mistake to judge a particular person's prophetic gift on the basis of one or two prophetic utterances. For one thing, all prophets need to grow and mature in their exercise of the gift—just as any other member of the body has to grow. Then too, it is usually not possible to determine the effectiveness of an individual's prophesying on the strength of a few experiences. Normally only a relatively long-term view will provide sufficient evidence to prove whether a prophet is fruitful or unfruitful in his services.

Submission to Authority

All these means of judging prophecy come together in the heads of the community. It is they who have the authority to determine whether or not an individual shall be allowed to prophesy. Furthermore, the elders have the authority to declare on behalf of the community that a particular prophecy is a word from the Lord. In other words, it is the heads who have the responsibility to discern and the authority to govern prophecy. They, and not the prophets, have the final word.

It is usually a mistake for prophets to be the ultimate authority in a group. A number of heterdox sects and groups have been led by "prophets," whose "inspired" statements led people astray. It is the place of the prophets to prophesy, but it is the place of the heads of the community to judge prophecy. Now of course this does not mean that prophets cannot also be heads in a community. Nor does it mean that a prophet cannot press his claims of inspiration in the face of adverse judgments by the heads of the community. It is entirely possible that the heads of a group could misuse their authority over prophecy—whether intentionally or unintentionally—and claim that something which is a true word from the Lord is false. In such a case the prophet can continue to proclaim that word, but only in submission to the heads. If the heads tell a prophet to cease publicly prophesying—then the prophet must submit. He can continue to speak privately to the heads about it, but he must abide by their decision to cease public proclamation.

In some ways, this is a hard word for the prophets. Yet in the order of the Christian community, the legitimate heads of the community must maintain their authority over all of the services within the community, and over its direction and response to the Lord. They cannot fulfill their role unless they are able to take full authority over the exercise of prophecy. Furthermore, it is to the heads of the church that Christ entrusts authority for determining what is true and what is false.

In short, the early church benefited from the tremendous resource of the prophetic gift, and yet avoided the dangers of false prophecy, by entrusting the final authority for determing the authenticity of prophecy to the heads of the community. The heads, in turn, based their judgment upon observation of the life of the prophet and the effects of his prophecy. When a truly spiritual man exhibited a gift for prophecy, a gift which produced life and power in the community, he was acknowledged to be a true prophet. The prophet was subject to the authority of the heads. But when the heads of the community discerned that a man truly spoke from God, they were submissive to the word he spoke. The prophet in the early church was a man of spiritual authority because of the gift God had assigned him. His authority was recognized and accepted because it was attested to by the authority of the church.

Notes

1. The claim to direct divine inspiration is both profound and disturbing. Many of us would like to alter that claim, to put prophecy

back in the realm of the purely human. In his book, *The Prophets,* Abraham Heschel cites several attempts by recent authors to modify the claims of direct divine inspiration in the Old Testament prophets. He quotes one, for instance, who states, "not seldom, when a prophet utters the words 'Thus saith the Lord!', his meaning might be expressed in a modern way, 'It is my profound conviction that such and such is God's thought (or will or purpose).' " But Heschel—very rightly—rejects such reductionist attempts. The claim to direct divine inspiration is crucial to the prophets. And that is true in the New Testament quite as much as in the Old. Heschel, *The Prophets,* Vol. II, p. 194 ff.

2. Cf., T. Dubay, *Caring* (Danville, New Jersey: Dimension Books, 1973), pp. 92-94, 96-98, 176. L. Duchesue, *Early History of the Christian Church,* Vol. I (London: J. Murray Co., 1909), pp. 34-38.

3. In this section I will refer to those who have the authority to regulate prophecy in the community as the "heads" of the community. In the early church those who had such authority were the *presbyteroi.* I, however, will use the term "heads" rather than any of the direct translations of *presbyteroi* (elders, presbyters, etc.) because my intention is not to discuss early church government, but to discuss prophecy.

4. Hermas, *The Shepherd,* Ante-Nicene Fathers, Vol. II (New York: The Christian Literature Co., 1890), pp. 27-28.

II

Growing in Prophetic Gifts

The first section of this book has dealt with prophecy as it ought to be in the church. This section will deal with "where we are now." I do not know of any Christian community which is in a position to approach prophecy just as described in Part I— and only a few which are close to being able to do so. Most groups and communities must begin at a different level and grow into maturity. The advice given here is intended to help people move toward a better understanding of prophecy and a better means of handling it in their own groups. This second section will therefore be much more practical and personal. This material is no less important than the preceding section. In some ways it is more important. If we do not lay a sure foundation in our actual practice right now the material in Part I will never be useful.

Chapter Five

Beginning to Prophesy

How well I remember my first prophecy!

In February, 1968—February eighteenth, to be exact—I attended a "Day of Renewal" in Williamston, Michigan. At that time, two hundred people would gather in Williamston every month from charismatic groups all over the state to spend a day praying and worshipping God.

The room was crowded and hot, the lighting a little too dim. But every face expressed the joy of being in God's presence. Almost every face, that is: I felt miserable. The meeting had begun as joyfully for me as for anyone, but after perhaps twenty minutes a simple thought had started to distract me. I had been distracted thousands of times before while trying to pray, but this was different. One simple thought had entered my mind and just would not go away. It kept running through my head over and over again.

That was problem enough, but I started to feel even worse when I realized that this simple thought sounded just like many prophecies. I had the unsettling sense that I was supposed to prophesy. It seemed ridiculous. I had never prophesied, knew nothing about prophesying. But the sense grew steadily stronger. It became a conviction: "This is God's word. Prophesy."

I explained to the Lord why I couldn't.

"Lord, I have never prophesied. I just know I'll botch it."

"Prophesy."

"But Lord, what if I make a mistake, and all of these inno-cent trusting people believe me? Why, I could be responsible for leading them down the wrong path. I know you don't want that."

"Prophesy."

I was getting more and more tense. I decided that I had better shift my tactics.

"It would be presumptuous. There are a lot of good, strong Christians here, and I'm just a baby in Christian life. I wouldn't dare presume to speak in your name. (I thought this last one was a clincher, because it sounded like a real virtue. Certainly God wouldn't want to make me lose my humility.)

"I've given you my word. Prophesy."

I played my trump card: outright refusal. "This is nonsense. I have just gotten over-excited. I am not going to prophesy, and that's that."

A couple of minutes later I prophesied. My simple, short prophetic message—a reassurance of God's love—came thun-dering out in a voice that might have sounded the call to judg-ment. And with that, all the tensions that had been building up took their toll: I actually passed out and had to be carried bodily from the room!

When I revived outside, I was sure that I had caused a disaster. Most of the people at the Day of Renewal had little experience of prophecy, and my dramatic delivery followed by physical collapse must have given them a bit too much "spiritual" excitement. I felt betrayed. When a friend came out to see how I was doing, I moaned, "Look what God did to me!" He laughed.

This all took place many years ago, when I was new to

prophecy and just plain young. Since that time we have all learned and matured. I can't say that I have ever seen anyone duplicate my rather extraordinary—and silly—performance. But I have watched others struggling with the same question that confronted me: How can I tell if I should prophesy?

The easiest way I know to answer that question is to return to the concept of a prophet as God's spokesman or messenger. If a king's official messenger were to go out and proclaim a message which the king had not written, he would be lying. And if another courtier—one who was not authorized to deliver royal messages—were to take even a true message and spread it about town, he would usurp the royal authority. In other words, any messenger must have two things before he can legitimately proclaim a message on behalf of another person: the message itself and the proper authorization to proclaim it.

Applied to prophecy, this precept means that a person must receive a message from God and God's authority to proclaim that message before he can prophesy.

As I discuss the ways we receive prophecies, I intend to speak in very practical terms. We cannot receive God's word if we think of that word as something abstract. In prophecy God himself speaks to us, but he speaks through ordinary men and women. My own first experience of prophecy may seem unexalted, even comical. But it was an experience of *prophecy*. It became comical because it came through me—an ordinary person who sometimes acts comically. Prophecy is a human experience, and we must discuss it in practical, human terms.

Receiving a Word From God

People can receive revelation for prophecy in different ways. Sometimes an individual may receive the actual words of a message. Or, he may receive a clear *sense* of what God wants to say without the actual words. And sometimes he may receive only the first word or two of a prophecy with the conviction that he should begin to speak.

Receiving the Words of a Message

The first way is the simplest to explain. While a group of people is praying together, one person may begin to feel that God wants to speak in prophecy. So he will ask the Lord to speak and turn his own attention to God as fully as possible. After a minute or so, some words or phrases or sentences may begin to go through his mind. Some people find this almost like listening to a tape recorded message—they seem to actually *hear* a voice speaking. Others find thoughts forming in their mind without any effort or direction of their own: the thoughts just come. However it happens, a complete message soon forms itself, and the person speaks out the words he has been given.

Often, when the Lord gives the precise words of a prophecy he has some very specific message to give. I have myself used words in prophecies that I had never before used. I recall an incident involving two friends of mine that shows just how specific the Lord can be.

Jerry Barker and his son Owen had come to Michigan from Texas to visit our community. While in Michigan, they had occasion to go to Detroit, and decided to spend a little time driving around to see the city.

They were particularly interested in visiting the inner-city because they came from an inner-city parish in Houston. Not knowing their way around Detroit, they prayed and asked God to direct them to the right place. As they prayed, two words came to Jerry's mind. Neither of the words meant anything to him. A few minutes later they turned off the expressway and went down a side-street. When they had stopped at an intersection, Jerry noticed, to his amazement, that the two streets that intersected bore the names that had come to his mind while they prayed! They parked the car and walked around for a while (it was in fact an inner-city neighborhood), looking at the area and praying for the people who lived there.

Several days later, back in Ann Arbor, Jerry and Owen were introduced to Rev. Ron Spann, the pastor of an Episcopal parish in inner-city Detroit. Ron listened to Jerry and Owen describe the work they had done in their own parish in Houston. Finally, he ventured to ask whether it would be at all possible for Jerry and Owen to move temporarily to Detroit to help with the work in his parish. In the course of the ensuing conversation Jerry told Ron of their experience in Detroit two days before. "The intersection you stopped at," Ron told them, "is in my parish. In fact, it's very close to the church. The people you were praying for are my parishioners." Eventually, Jerry and his wife and several others did move to Detroit from Houston. The work which they later did in Detroit is, I think, evidence that it was indeed the Lord who had first guided them there.

Incidents like this do not happen to each of us every day. Most of the times when we receive the actual words of prophecy directly the words are not unusual or unfamiliar to us. But God can still have a specific purpose in his choice of words. Often, more than one person will receive the same prophecy. On many occasions I have heard people prophesy a message exactly as I heard it from the Lord myself—word for word the same. Occurrences like that can build up our confidence in the prophetic gift.

When we receive a prophetic message in this way, we should take care to speak the message exactly as we receive it; neither adding to nor taking away from the words which the Lord gives. To paraphrase Ezekiel 3:17, "When you hear a word from my mouth—just say it."

Receiving the Sense of a Message

Many times when we receive a prophecy, we will not receive specific words to speak. Instead, we will be given a very clear sense of the message God wants spoken. By "a sense of the message," I mean more than a general idea of what God wants to say. I mean a clear, even a precise, understanding of the specific message the Lord is giving.

How does this work?

When we speak with others in normal conversation, we rarely rehearse everything we intend to say. We only put our thoughts into words as we begin to speak. But because we understand clearly what we want to say, we know when we are expressing ourselves correctly. Again, when we sing a familiar song, we do not rehearse all of the lyrics in our mind before singing them. We simply begin to sing, knowing that the words will come because we know the song.

Many times when I feel that the Lord wants to speak, I receive a clear understanding of the message, but do not immediately know how to say it. So I must supply the right words for the message myself. Because I do have a *clear* sense of the message, I can tell when I have discovered the correct way to express it. I can then confidently say "This is the word the Lord wants to speak." I don't say "This is *like* the message the Lord wants to speak," but "This *is* the message the Lord wants to speak."

Receiving the First Words of a Message

People who prophesy will sometimes receive neither the words nor the sense of the message. Instead, they will receive only a word or two. If they are convinced that those few words begin a full prophetic message, they can simply begin to speak out. As they do so, the rest of the message will be given to them.

This experience of prophecy is perhaps the most common for people who are just beginning to prophesy. A person needs a certain amount of courage to go ahead and speak when all he has to say is the beginning of one sentence. His obedience will, however, be rewarded.

A good friend of mine in another prayer group had an interesting experience along these lines. During a prayer meeting eight years ago, when prophecy was still very new to him, this man began to sense that he should prophesy. But the only words that came to him were "the owl in the night"! Inwardly he groaned. "How will it sound if I say 'Thus says the Lord, The owl in the night . . . says the Lord.' " He could not bring himself to do anything so ridiculous. But as the minutes went by he became more and more convinced that he really should prophesy, even though he had still not received anything more than that one absurd phrase. Finally, he opened his mouth and began. To his surprise (and relief) those words were the beginning of a truly beautiful, poetic message from the Lord.

Whether I receive the exact wording or a sense of a prophetic message, or only receive the first few words, if I am faithful in speaking the word I have been given, the message I speak will be a true word from the Lord. Prophecy can be impure—our own thoughts or ideas can get mixed into the message we receive—whether we receive all the words directly or only receive a sense of the message. Later, I will explain ways we can test prophecy to determine what is truly from God and what is not. But even though prophecy may sometimes be impure (and Paul says that all our prophecy is imperfect) we can learn through prayer and experience to become increasingly faithful to the message God wishes to speak.

Receiving the Authority to Prophesy

The spirit which had lifted me up seized me, and I went off spiritually stirred, while the hand of the Lord rested heavily upon me.

(Ezek. 3:14)

Ezekiel describes an experience which many contemporary Christian prophets will easily recognize: "The spirit seized me . . . I was spiritually stirred . . . the hand of the Lord rested heavily upon me." In prophecy the Spirit of God stirs a person up, urges him to speak, burns like a fire in his bones. This experience may be tranquil and restful, or turbulent, powerful, exciting. But it always carries with it peace and a sense of God's presence.

On the day I gave my traumatic first prophecy, I experienced both an urging to speak the message I had heard, and a conviction that the Holy Spirit himself was urging me. In all my experiences with prophecy since that time, I have felt both that urging and that conviction. All the experiences of prophecy I have ever heard others describe or read about in Scripture contain those two elements—an urge to speak a message that has been received and the conviction that the message and the urgency both come from the Holy Spirit.

For those who dislike or mistrust spiritual experience I can offer little consolation here. Nothing will ever help you to prophesy if you cannot acknowledge the experience of being commissioned by God to speak his word. You can test a prophecy after it has been given without getting involved in a spiritual experience, but you can never give a prophecy unless you have a prophetic experience.

Much of the current writing on Christian prophecy talks about being "anointed" to prophesy. The term "anointing" is taken from the Old Testament, where it describes a sacred ceremony used to dedicate a person for some special service. For example, oil was poured over the head of a king to signify that he had been authorized to rule. The book of Isaiah speaks of a person who has been "anointed" to bring good news to the poor. In Christian literature, this term "anointing" often describes the action of the Holy Spirit as he prepares and empowers a person to preach or perform some miraculous work. Many people will more readily recognize the term "unction," taken from the Latin word for anointing.

In reference to prophecy, "anointing" describes the Holy Spirit's action in commissioning and empowering a person to speak prophetically. "To receive an anointing to prophesy" means to experience an urging to speak a prophetic message and the conviction that the message is from God.

Sometimes an anointing involves physical experience as well as inner conviction. Many people describe feeling a tingling sensation on their back or lips just before they speak in prophecy. Others experience tightness in the chest or an "elevator" feeling in the pit of the stomach, or the sensation of wind blowing over their hands. Whatever the feeling, this physical sensation is not in itself an anointing to prophesy; the sensation merely *accompanies* the interior action of the Holy Spirit. In fact, if we pay too much attention to the physical sensations, we can get confused.

For two years after I first began to experience the gift of prophecy, I felt physical sensations like those described above every time I prophesied. I began to equate those sensations with the actual anointing to speak in prophecy. Then, suddenly, they ceased. I just did not experience any physical sensations at all. But I still felt an urging to prophesy; in fact I felt an even greater conviction that I should prophesy than I had before. For a month or two this new situation confused me: I was never sure whether to prophesy or not. My dilemma ended when I spoke with a man who had been prophesying for a long time. He told me that he sometimes felt physical signs as part of an anointing and sometimes didn't, but that he always experienced a conviction that the Holy Spirit wanted him to speak.

Physical sensations are not at all reliable, and we should never depend on them to tell us whether or not to prophesy. If physical signs occur, that's fine. It's also fine if they never occur at all.

The commissioning or anointing of a person to prophesy is a

"spiritual experience," but by that I do not mean an event involving only a person's feelings. Most modern men assume that a spiritual experience is a purely internal and subjective event. But prophetic inspiration goes far beyond that. It is an encounter with a concrete, living reality—the person of God. The term "spiritual experience" may be too weak to describe this, because it can hide the objective reality of the event. The fact that a prophet knows that he or she has encountered something outside of himself—namely, God and his word—is crucial to an understanding of prophetic inspiration or "anointing."[1]

No one can ever achieve, all on his own, a complete certainty that God has given him a message to speak. But with time and the help of other Christians, he can come to a real confidence in his sensitivity to the promptings of the Holy Spirit. The work of the Spirit in prophecy is not elusive. We do not exercise the gift of prophecy in the shadow of doubt, but in the clear knowledge that God is *eager* to reveal to us his word.

Prophetic Language

Two years ago I spoke at a conference in Puerto Rico. The conference participants prayed together often and heard the Lord speak through prophecy. At the beginning of the first session I was surprised to hear the leader of the conference, Fr. Tom Forrest, request that everyone pray and prophesy in English. Most people in Puerto Rico speak both English and Spanish, but since these meetings involved many North Americans, English had been chosen as the official language of the conference. I had not realized before that people could choose to prophesy in one language over another. However, an incident back in my own community a few years earlier had indicated that this might be so.

Our community consists of people from different church backgrounds who customarily read different versions of the

Bible. At the time I am speaking of, some of the people who used the King James Version always prophesied in archaic-sounding English. Everyone else prophesied in normal modern English. For instance, one person might prophesy, "Verily I say, am I not among you?" while another would simply say, "I am among you."

Most of the people in the community had difficulty understanding prophecies given in the archaic language so I asked the people concerned to use normal English instead. They were amazed at my request. "Shouldn't we prophesy whatever God gives us?"

The language we use in prophecy is under our control. Prophecy comes through a *particular* human being, and it will be expressed in the language of that person. When a highly educated man speaks in prophecy, he will very likely use a different vocabulary than a poorly educated person would use. In the same way, when a child prophesies the prophecy will usually be stated in a child's words.

We are responsible for the language we use in prophecy. The whole purpose of prophecy is to bring God's word to his people. If no one can understand what we say, our prophesying will not fulfill that purpose. When the people in our community spoke in archaic English, their language actually got in the way of God's word. They had to change the way they spoke.

We can be attentive to the language we use in prophecy even if we receive only the first few words of the message. In day to day life, we normally modify the way we talk according to our surroundings. When relaxing with our friends, we can be quite casual—leave sentences incomplete, use colloquialisms, even throw in some slang. But during an interview for a job, we speak more formally. We won't usually "compose" everything said in a job interview, but we will let our need for more presentable speech guide us. Prophecy can work the very same way. If we know that we should use clear and direct speech, that knowledge can guide the way we prophesy—even if we do not "rehearse" the prophecy in our minds beforehand.

At times special rhetorical devices can help make a prophetic word more powerful and effective. Isaiah spoke poetically and at times even composed songs to convey the Lord's word. Many of the prophets used images and allegories to embellish their words. As we mature in exercising the prophetic gift, we might find ways to use some of these devices ourselves. But normally, we need only be concerned to speak God's word in a simple and straightforward way. I have not yet heard a prophecy fail to communicate the Lord's message because it was cast in simple everyday language. I have, however, heard people trying so hard to use beautiful language that they failed to express God's word. We don't need beautiful language—we need God's word. When we have grown in the Christian life and in the prophetic gift we may be able to prophesy beautifully as well as clearly. But our first concern should be clarity.[2]

To put it all simply, we should prophesy in a way that will help others understand the Lord's word. If the Lord gives us particular words to use, we should just speak them out as we receive them. If we have to supply our own words, we should keep them simple and clear. We don't need to be great poets; we need only speak God's word.

Delivering the Prophetic Message

Imagine a king who wishes to proclaim a solemn message to his subjects. He carefully composes the message, making sure that what he says can easily be understood. He chooses an ideal day for proclaiming the message, and has his most trusted messenger dressed in royal robes and escorted to the town square by guards and trumpeters. The people assemble in the square, the messenger mounts the platform amid blasts of the horns. A deep quiet falls over the crowd. The messenger un-rolls the scroll, clears his throat, and then *mumbles* the message! He turns and walks back to the castle unheard.

Or imagine that the messenger takes the message and walks to the city gate. There, with all solemnity, he reads the royal decree—while all the people are waiting back in the town square.

In either case I suppose the king would at least fire the messenger.

The way a message is proclaimed, and the time and the place, matter just as much in prophesying as in delivering royal proclamations. We need to observe a few, simple guidelines that will help us get the prophetic word to the ears of those for whom it is intended.

First of all, we must speak so that people can hear us. If a person prophesies in a very quiet voice to a large group, no one will hear the prophecy. On the other hand, if someone roars out a message in a small group, people may be too startled to hear what is said. Match the way that you speak to the situation that you are in. If you have to stand up or use a microphone to be heard, then do so. If you have a tendency to speak very forcefully, then you may at times have to take care not to overpower those who are listening.

Secondly, we should prophesy in the appropriate place and at the right time. I know a man who felt that he had received a prophetic word while attending a service in his church. So he prophesied. Most members of that congregation had never heard a prophecy before and had no idea what that man was doing. His prophecy only produced confusion and embarrassment.

From time to time we will receive a word from the Lord, and even feel urged to speak it, at an inappropriate time or place. When that happens, we should not prophesy. Paul's statement that "the spirits of prophets are under the prophets' control," carries a very important truth. We have to exercise some care for the gift of prophecy; at times we even have to decide whether we should prophesy.

I learned this lesson when attending a conference several years ago. Most of those who attended the conference were familiar with the gift of prophecy, as were the conference speakers. One day, right in the middle of a talk, a woman spoke out from the audience in prophecy. Of course the speaker, the Rev. Graham Pulkingham, stopped for a few moments to let her finish prophesying. Then Fr. Pulkingham told her, firmly but gently, that she should not have prophesied in the middle of a talk. The woman took no offense at his correction, and I think everyone present benefited from the instruction.

It would be a little easier for us, I suppose, if we did not have to take responsibility for our exercise of the gift of prophecy. We could just say "Well, God gave me the prophecy, so blame it on him if things didn't quite work out." But God has committed his gifts to our hands, and we have to learn how to administer them for his sake. Rather than complain, we should thank God that he has allowed us to serve him. And then we should exert ourselves to serve him more and more responsibly.

Notes

1. For the scientific mind, testimony to an experience is not acceptable unless it can be verified. Prophetic experience can be verified, and a later chapter is devoted to verification of prophecy. The mistake of "scientific" verification of spiritual experience usually lies in the criteria applied. That a person can have an objective encounter with God is never allowed as a possiblity. But verification of prophecy—or any discussion of prophecy at all—presupposes that

a person *can* have an objective encounter with God. That is to say, it presupposes faith.

2. "The prophet, on the other hand, definitely knows what his utterance implies. The intention is more important than the impression. His purpose is not to elaborate his views artistically, but to set them forth effectively. *His primary concern is the message rather than the form.*" Heschel, op. cit., II, 168 (italics mine)

Chapter Six

The Forms of Prophecy

Let me now sing of my friend
  my friend's song concerning his
  vineyard.

(Isa. 5:1)

(Agabus) came up to us and taking Paul's belt, tied his own hands and feet with it. Then he said, "Thus says the Holy Spirit . . ."

(Acts 21:10)

The prophets of both the Old and New Testaments did a great deal more to communicate the word of the Lord than just saying "Thus says the Lord." They composed songs (or sang songs inspired by the Holy Spirit), they performed dramatic actions—they even gave their children prophetic names:

"In fact, they showed no hesitation in availing themselves of all manner of forms in which to clothe their message. None, secular and sacred alike, was safe from appropriation as a vessel for discharge of his task by one prophet or another."[1]

Oracles

The simplest and most direct form of prophecy is the prophetic oracle, in which the prophet addresses the people of God in plain speech as if it were the Lord himself speaking. A prophetic oracle may or may not contain such idioms as "The Lord says" or "The Holy Spirit says this." But whether or not these familiar prophetic phrases are employed, it is clear from the speaker's presentation that the speech proceeds from the Lord.

Oracles are blunt. They state the message of the Lord without elaborate presentation. Therein lies their greatest usefulness. There are occasions (frequent occasions) which call for the simple statement of the message God has for his people. Prophetic oracles present a direct word as a direct word, and state simply that "this word is from the Lord."

Prophetic Exhortation

Perhaps the most common form of prophetic speech is exhortation. The fifteenth chapter of the book of Acts mentions two prophets, Judas and Silas, who came to Antioch and "exhorted the brethren with many words, and strengthened them." Exhortation (or encouragement as it is often translated) is speech which revives, renews, or strengthens people. It builds up their hope and gives them new courage. Most of us are familiar with exhortation, although we probably have not called it that. The well-known halftime pep talk which the coach gives his team, for instance, is exhortation.

Any Christian can exhort and encourage other Christians. If someone were anxious and worried about his financial state, any good Christian could encourage him to have faith in God, who provides more abundantly for us than for the sparrows. But there is a true *prophetic* exhortation too, and prophetic exhortation is something more: it is *inspired* by the Holy

Spirit. It is a word of encouragement that comes from the Lord himself.

About three years ago Ralph Martin addressed a gathering at the "Michigan Day of Rededication." The people attending had all been serving God for years and were suffering the weariness that naturally follows long labor. Ralph's talk, "The Joyful Suffering of a Faithful Servant" was a clear and powerful exhortation to keep on in the service of the Lord. People who left that gathering knew they had heard God's word. They felt refreshed and eager to return to their service.

Oftentimes we may know that the Lord wants to say something to his people, yet do not feel that we should prophesy. In such cases, we should perhaps yield to an inspired exhortation. In some ways, inspired exhortation allows us greater freedom for expression than direct, first-person prophecy. We can communicate the Lord's word at greater length or in more detail than is otherwise possible. We can express our own convictions about the Lord's word or use personal examples to explain how the word can be applied. Just two weeks before writing this chapter I attended a gathering of Christians from my home town. As we were praying together, I felt inspired to speak a prophetic word. But when I considered the message, I realized that a story I had just read could express it better than a first-person prophecy. So, rather than prophesying, I gave a prophetic exhortation, including the story as an illustration.

If you ever feel that the Lord wishes to speak through you, but direct prophecy does not appear to be the right way to communicate his word, try expressing it through a prophetic exhortation. Some people fear that speaking an exhortation rather than a prophecy will weaken the force of God's word—perhaps people will think we are only expressing some personal convictions. If we believe our exhortation is God's word, we can simply say that. If it is, our words will carry God's authority.

Inspired Prayer

At times God will inspire a person to pray publicly in a way that touches and moves the hearts of those who hear. At times too the prayer will have in it the unmistakable element of prophetic revelation. When Zechariah and Symeon prayed in thanks to God (see Luke, chapters 1 and 2), their prayers were thoroughly prophetic. Through those prayers God revealed the plan he was unfolding in John the Baptist and Jesus.

Prophetic prayer often has a place in worship of the Lord. Ezra 9:6-15 and Nehemiah 9:6-37 are examples of prophetic prayer. When Ezra prayed before the people, the people were deeply affected. His prayer had power because it was inspired. A truly inspired prayer will turn people's hearts to the Lord, and will lead them to a deep praise and worship of God. When inspired prayer is present, worship of God is a powerful and transforming experience.

Prophetic prayer is as easy to yield to as direct prophecy. If you are praying and feel that the Lord has given you something to pray publicly, just speak out, and let the power of the Holy Spirit do the rest.

Prophecy in Song

Some of the most beautiful and moving melodies and lyrics I have heard were prophetic. Prophetic songs most often occur in the context of worship, and serve as an encouragement to even greater praise of God. Many of these songs describe God's goodness, his love, or his majesty, in a way which almost compels us to bless God and praise him.

Receiving a prophetic song is similar to receiving a simple prophetic message. Sometimes you will begin to hear in your mind a word from the Lord, and melody along with it. Other times you may receive only the words of a prayer or message, but feel urged to *sing* the message rather than to speak it.

When that happens, if you just choose an opening note and begin to sing, the melody will come. Or, you may receive only a melody, but as you begin to sing, the words will be given to you. Prophetic song does not come when you decide to set something to music, but when you are inspired to sing in the Holy Spirit. In other words, you don't *compose* a prophetic song, you *receive* it.

The words of a prophetic song are not so much a focus as the words of a spoken prophecy. Prophetic song *usually* communicates an experience, or stirs us up spiritually, in somewhat the same way prayer or exhortation does.

Normally prophetic song will be given to people who have a good singing voice. God uses the natural gifts which he gives to us to support the spiritual gifts which he bestows. If you do have a good singing voice you should be open to receiving from the Lord a prophecy in song. But keep in mind that there are surprises in the ways of the Lord. Maybe you don't think that you can sing at all. Well, I have heard some people who couldn't carry a tune sing beautifully under the inspiration of the Holy Spirit. I have also heard people who have been trained in voice try to sing prophecy with embarrassing results. It helps to know that God *normally* uses our natural gifts; but that shouldn't keep us from receiving any gift which he wants to give.

Revelation

When Jesus told the woman at the well (John 4) that she had had five husbands, and was now living with a man who was not her husband, she replied, "Sir, I perceive that you are a prophet." That reply would have come naturally to most people at the time of Jesus. They knew that a prophet could bring hidden things to light and lay bare the secrets of the heart. Scripture abounds with accounts of prophets who revealed secrets they could never have known except through the action of the Holy Spirit. To cite one example, the prophet Elisha knew that his servant Gehazi had lied to get money from a man whom Elisha had cured (2 Kings 5).

From time to time God may reveal things to us which we could not otherwise know, just as he revealed Gehazi's theft to Elisha. Four years ago I was counseling a young woman troubled by serious emotional difficulties. I knew that the Lord wanted to help her, but I myself was at a loss about what to do. At the beginning of one session, we sat down to pray together. As we prayed the Lord showed me an incident involving a small child and her mother. I saw the incident in very great detail, almost as if a movie was being shown in my mind. A girl who appeared to be about four years old was sitting in her living room playing with some toys. Suddenly her mother came into the room and began to yell at her. She spanked the girl severely and sent her to her room. As I saw all of this, I understood (how I am not sure) that the little girl had been wetting her bed at night. Her mother was angry because it had happened again. The little girl was bewildered, frightened, and frustrated. I understood (again, I don't know how) that she felt helpless: how could she control what happened in her sleep?

I was a little nervous about mentioning this, but I finally worked up the courage. I told the woman that I thought something had happened between her and her mother when she was about four years old. As I described what I had seen, she became more and more excited. The revelation was an exact description of an incident she had almost forgotten. Every detail matched. Talking about that spanking given many years before led us to some insights that eventually helped her overcome some of her emotional problems.

Revelation of facts which we could not know on our own can be a powerful and convincing work of the Holy Spirit. The woman at the well came to believe in Jesus because he knew things about her that he could never have known except through God's revelation. Paul says in his first letter to the

Corinthians, "If all prophesy, and an unbeliever or outsider enters, he is convicted by all, he is called to account by all; the secrets of his heart are disclosed; and so, falling on his face he will worship God and declare that God is really among you" (1 Cor. 14:24-25).

However, we must be careful to use these revelations in a way that will help and encourage the people involved. This is especially true of revelations concerning people's private lives. Such revelations can cause tremendous harm if they are rashly or unlovingly used. Several years ago I was praying with another person, and as I prayed, God showed me something that had happened to him many years before. This revelation touched on a very delicate matter, and I felt it unwise to bring the subject up. So I said nothing. One year later I talked with the same person, and he began to speak about the very incident that had been revealed to me a year earlier. I now thank God that I did not say anything about that revelation when I first received it. God had a time and a place for making use of the knowledge he had given me.

There are two areas in which we need to exercise care with prophetic revelation. First, we may be *wrong* when we think that something has been revealed to us. Second, it is not always appropriate or helpful to say anything about the true revelations which we receive.

We could be wrong. Imagine what would happen if you walked up to a woman who had been faithfully married for fifteen years and said, "You have had five husbands and you are now living with a man who is not your husband." When we receive true revelation, we may become the instruments of a dramatic conversion. But when we have "received" something false, we can only hurt, offend, or embarrass another individual. The more serious the matter which we think has been revealed, the more serious is our responsibilty to discern and judge it. We must always be prudent about such matters.

Again, God may give us a true revelation, but not want us to act on it. He may be revealing something just so we can pray and wait for him to act. I do believe, however, that most of the time when God shows us something, he will also show us what he wants us to do. If we seek for his guidance about how to act (or not act) on the revelation we receive, we can avoid mistakes.

God wants to equip us to serve him, and revelations can be an important part of that equipment. But they have to be approached with caution and wisdom. If we exercise a reasonable amount of care and common sense, revelation can bear fruit for the Lord.

Personal Prophecy

The Lord can speak through prophecy to individuals just as he can to groups of people. Through Agabus (and many others) the Holy Spirit warned Paul of the troubles awaiting him in Jerusalem. From time to time we may also experience the Lord giving us a specific word for some other individual. The word may give direction to someone who is trying to make a decision; it may encourage or console; it may convict a person of sin, as Nathan's prophecy convicted David of his sin in killing Bathsheba's husband (2 Sam. 12).

My own first experience with prophecy for another individual is worth relating, because it demonstrates the powerful effects that such prophecy can have. As I was praying one morning six years ago, I looked up and saw another man sitting across the room. I knew this man rather well, and there was nothing unusual about seeing him in the room, for he often prayed there. But as I looked at him that morning, I sensed that the Lord had something to speak to him. I went over to him and told him that I thought I should prophesy to him. He looked a bit surprised. The prophecy which I spoke was very simple: God knew him and loved him. Later that day this man came to me to thank me for the prophecy. The knowledge that God loved him—loved him enough to speak to him personally—had a profound effect. Two years later he again thanked me for what I had done that day. That simple word had been for him a support and encouragement through many difficult times. Often, he told me, it would come back to his mind in the midst of trials and bring with it an inner strength and refreshment.

At times prophecy for individuals can be misused. I have heard of instances where people have made use of personal "prophecy" as a means for getting their own way. For instance, one person "prophesied" to another person that God wanted the two of them to get married. Apparently he wanted his proposal to have some authority behind it! Prophecy for an individual is subject to the same need for testing and discernment as any other form of prophecy. If a prophecy requires some definite response, then it should be examined and judged, whether it is intended for a group or for an individual.

Visions

For many of us the archetypical prophet may be John on the Island of Patmos:

> And after this I looked, and lo, in heaven an open door! And the first voice, which I had heard speaking to me like a trumpet said, "Come up hither and I will show you what must take place after this." At once I was in the Spirit, and, lo, a throne stood in heaven, with one seated on the throne! And he who sat there appeared like jasper and carnelian, and round the throne there was a rainbow that look like an emerald. . . .
>
> (Rev. 4:1-3)

Or it may be Ezekiel:

> In the thirtieth year, in the fourth month, on the fifth day
> of the month, as I was among the exiles by the river
> Chebar, the heavens were opened and I saw visions of
> God. . . .
>
> (Ezek. 1:1)

Probably nothing else makes us feel so different from the
prophets, so alienated from their experience, as the visions
they received. Visons seem to have about them an air of unre-
ality and mystery and spectacle. And yet visions are no more
mysterious than normal prophecy. Actually, they ought to be
expected.

Through visions God opens up to us his action and his plan
in a new and powerful way; they have impact. I was startled,
to say the least, the first time I received a vision. After all, I
considered myself a reasonable and down-to-earth sort of guy.
And I didn't think any reasonable and down-to-earth person
should allow himself to have visions!

But in the summer of 1969, while I was on retreat with a
group of men in Canada, I had a vision. We were all praying
together one night, and I felt that the Lord wished to speak to
us through prophecy. I began seeking the Lord to hear his
word. Suddenly, I seemed to be standing on a large level plain.
A huge crowd of people was walking toward me. I could not
see any leader, but all the people were moving along together
as if following someone. The question I had read many times
in the books of the prophets immediately came to my lips,
"Lord, what is this?" I think, in fact, that I actually asked the
question half out loud because at that moment I was not particularly aware of the other people in the room. Then I heard
the Lord speaking, just as he normally does in prophetic revelation: "These are my people. They follow me where I lead
. . ."

In a minute or two the vision ended. What was I to do next? Tell people that I had had a vision? So much for my reputation as a reasonable and down-to-earth guy! But I plucked up my courage and said, "Ah, brothers, I think I've . . . uh . . . had a vision?" As I went on to explain what I had seen and heard, the other men responded just as they would respond to the word of the Lord in a spoken prophecy.

If we receive prophetic visions, we should share them with others properly. There is no reason to act as if something very strange or mysterious has happened: we can simply give a matter-of-fact description of what we have seen and heard. The vision can then be tested and judged as any other prophecy is tested and judged. If it is from God, it will bear the testing.

We should also talk about visions with dignity and restraint. I was tempted to half joke about my first vision, because I felt slightly embarrassed by it. But if a vision is from the Lord, embarrassment or joking will take away from what he wishes to do through it.

I have a relatively active imagination, and when I first experienced visions I thought I might be imagining them. That is a reasonable consideration: many people do mistake their own active and colorful imaginings for prophetic vision. But though such mistakes do occur, they mean only that we must apply the same tests to visions that we apply to every other form of prophecy. People who are emotionally unstable or prone to imagining things should not be relied upon in prophecy at all. We should know that a person is reliable before we accept his visions.

Prophetic Actions

Thus the Lord said to me: "Make yourself thongs and yoke-bars, and put them on your neck. Send word to the king of Edom, the king of Moab . . ."

(Jer. 27:2-3)

While we were staying for some days, a prophet named
Agabus came down from Judea. And coming to us he took
Paul's girdle and bound his own hands and feet and said,
"Thus says the Holy Spirit, 'So shall the Jews at
Jerusalem bind the man who owns this girdle and deliver
him into the hands of the Gentiles.' "

(Acts 21:10-11)

The prophets of both the Old and the New Testaments
brought drama and impact to their prophecies by performing,
under the inspiration of the Holy Spirit, actions that vividly
portrayed the message they proclaimed. Hosea and Isaiah
gave their children prophetic names (Hos. 1:4, 6,9; Isa. 8:3).
Ezekiel built a model of Jerusalem under siege (Ezek. 4:1-3).
Jeremiah, the champion prophetic actor, buried a waistcloth
(13:1), smashed an earthen flask as a sign of destruction (10),
walked around wearing an oxen-yoke (27), and bought a field
as a sign of future restoration (32).

All of these actions were *inspired* dramatizations of the
prophetic message. The prophets did not perform them because they wanted to be dramatic; they performed them at the
word of the Lord. Today we can see many people performing
what they claim are prophetic actions—burning draft files,
holding demonstrations, etc. In a broad sense of the term, we
might justly call these actions "prophetic symbols." But acting at the immediate command of the Lord in support of an
inspired prophetic message is a different matter. The power of
truly prophetic actions comes from the Holy Spirit who inspires them.

Tongues and Interpretation

Therefore he who speaks in tongues should pray for the
power to interpret. . . . If any speak in a tongue, let there
be two or at most three, and each in turn; and let one

interpret. But if there is no one to interpret, let each of them keep silence in the assembly and speak to himself and to God.

(1 Cor. 14:13, 27-28)

Paul spoke very strongly to the church at Corinth about speaking in tongues in meetings of the church. Speaking out in tongues was to be done only if the message spoken could be interpreted. The reason Paul gives is common sense: unless the message is interpreted, no one will understand it, and therefore, no one will profit from the message. It is clear that at times the Holy Spirit does inspire individuals to speak out in tongues in Christian meetings. When the message spoken is interpreted, all are "built up."

I have been asked on many occasions "Why should God inspire tongues and interpretation? Wouldn't it be simpler for someone to just speak the message in an intelligible language in the first place?" I do not have an answer for a question like that. It seems clear that God *does* inspire tongues and interpretation. It would be better for us simply to exercise and receive the gift with thanksgiving than to ask why God works in this way.

One prominent Pentecostal writer maintains that when tongues are spoken and interpreted, the interpretation should be an inspired prayer. Tongues, he explains, is a gift for prayer, and so the interpreted message ought logically to be an inspired prayer. There is real merit to this argument, but my experience and the experience of many other Christians seems to indicate that at least sometimes a message in tongues will be interpreted not as a prayer, but as a prophecy.

Tongues with interpretation operates in much the same way as the gift of prophecy. One individual will feel "anointed" to speak out. But rather than receiving a message to speak, he will feel urged to speak out in an unknown tongue. The individual who then receives the interpretation will also feel

⋅"anointed" to speak, and will receive from God either a message or the beginnings of a message. Most often he will also feel a conviction that the message he has received interprets the message spoken in tongues.[2]

I firmly believe that tongues and interpretation *ought* to operate in the church. Many of us seem to find this gift less "rational" and therefore more embarrassing than simple prophecy. But I have seen tongues and interpretation bring life and power to God's people. It is part of the prophetic gift given to the church, and we should look for it, expect to experience it, and receive it with thanks.

Prophecy in Private Prayer

Five years ago I had a brief conversation with someone who told me that while he was praying by himself, he had felt "anointed" to prophesy. He had felt a little uneasy about this, since there was no one around to hear his prophecy, but he finally prophesied anyway. The word that God spoke inspired him greatly.

I went away scratching my head and feeling a bit suspicious. "Prophecy," I thought to myself, "is a gift given for the body of Christ. It is meant for others, not for yourself, right? Then how can someone prophesy while he is all alone?" But a few months later, as I was praying alone, I felt that *I* should prophesy. I did, and I too found myself greatly inspired and encouraged by God's message.

Since that time I have often prophesied while praying by myself and have come to believe that it is quite normal. True, prophecy is a gift given to the body of Christ, but there is no reason why the Lord cannot use that gift to speak directly to individuals, to encourage them, to lead them in worship.

If you ever feel that you should prophesy while praying alone, yield to it and speak out the prophecy. When I first experienced prophecy in this way I thought, "I already know what the Lord is saying to me, so why should I prophesy?" The reason is simple: prophecy is a spoken word. When we speak the message God gives, the power of the prophetic gift becomes active.

One word of caution. It is very hard to test a prophecy given when no one else is present to judge it. Accordingly, we should not rely on these prophecies for guidance or direction.

All the manifestations of the prophetic gift can bring life to God's people. Each kind of prophetic speech adds its own depth and scope and texture and beauty to the manifestation of God's word. Few people will have occasion to use all these types of prophecy, but anyone who is called to speak God's word will very likely find that his word can take at least several different forms.

Notes

1. Von Rad, *Old Testament Theology,* p. 38.
2. See George Montague's explanation of this gift in *The Spirit and His Gifts* (New York: Paulist Press, 1974), pp. 33-35.

Chapter Seven

The Discernment of Prophecy

In the twenty second chapter of the first book of Kings we read of a dispute between the prophet Micaiah and four hundred prophets of Israel. The king of Israel had asked them all whether he should fight against the Syrians for possession of a border town named Ramoth-Gilead. Four hundred prophets promised the king victory if he attacked the Syrians. Micaiah said that he would be defeated. Micaiah was right. Israel lost the battle and their king was killed.

The prophet Jeremiah had a similar encounter with another prophet named Hananiah (Jer. 28). Jeremiah had been prophesying to Judah that it was hopeless for them to fight against Babylon. Instead, said Jeremiah, they should submit themselves to Babylon or they would be destroyed. Hananiah, on the other hand, prophesied that the Babylonians would not rule over the land of Judah. The two men had a "prophetic battle" in which it appeared that Hananiah came out on top. But Jeremiah insisted that he had a true word from the Lord, and that Hanaiah would die within a year because he had prophesied falsely. Several months later Hananiah died, and shortly after the Babylonians utterly destroyed Jerusalem.

Both of these incidents point to a question of great concern: How can we know what is truly a word from the Lord? (cf., chapter 4.)

The question is an important one. God's people can be led astray if they do not take care to distinguish true prophecy from false. Many times in the past men who claimed to have a word from the Lord have used their prestige to corrupt the truth. Jesus even said this would happen:

> If anyone tells you at that time, "Look the messiah is here," or "He is there," do not believe it. False messiahs and false prophets will appear, performing signs and wonders so great as to mislead even the chosen if that were possible.
>
> (Matt. 24:24)

> Be on your guard against false prophets, who come to you in sheep's clothing, but underneath are ravening wolves.
>
> (Matt. 7:15)

Many Christians shy away from all prophecy because of the dangers of false prophets. But that is a serious mistake. The people of God need to hear God's voice in prophecy. Paul warned the Thessalonians: "Do not stifle the Spirit. Do not despise prophecies. Test everything; retain what is good" (1 Thess. 5:19-21).

In other words, we should not stop giving prophecies; we should test our prophecies, and hold on only to those which are good. We need not approach prophecy with fear or even great caution. We do need to approach it with faith and with wisdom.

Faith first of all. If we do not expect to hear God speaking, we will not hear him. If we do not *desire* God's word in prophecy, and *believe* that prophecy will come, it will not come. We must build a climate of faith if we are to receive all that God is willing to give. Jesus could not perform any mighty works in one Galilean town because the people there lacked faith (Mark 6:1-6). God works when we believe in him. He speaks when we are confident that he will speak to us.

At one time several years ago I seemed to be completely unable to prophesy. I would pray and seek for God's words but to no avail. Many others in the community experienced the very same thing; prophecy seemed almost to disappear. Then we began to notice that many community members were not expecting to hear the Lord speaking through prophecy. The "level of faith" in the community had apparently reached low ebb. When we worked to build the community's faith back up, the prophetic gift became active again. When our hearts were filled with expectant faith, the word of the Lord came to us in abundance.

Once the prophetic gifts are operating freely, we need to develop the wisdom to judge the true from the false and the pure from the corrupt.

The Good and the Bad

False prophecy is not the only kind of bad prophecy. By false prophecy I mean something which is truly extraordinary, but which does not come from the Spirit of God. Jesus warned against false prophets who would perform wonders. False prophets have a real extraordinary power, but it does not come from God. The spirit behind it is evil. A number of people today who claim to be prophets exhibit some real spiritual power—forecasting events and even performing miracles or "psychic phenomena." Yet it is a serious, even fatal, mistake to be led along by them. We should always ask ourselves, "Is this from the Lord? Does it proceed from the Holy Spirit and glorify God?" The exponents of Edgar Cayce, various forms of mind control, and other cults all claim to exhibit spiritual powers, and often do. The question is, what spirit does their power come from?

Prophecy can be "bad," however, without being false. Sometimes people will speak in a prophetic manner when they are in fact only voicing their own thoughts. Other times people will speak a true prophetic word, but will mix in with it some of their own ideas which don't belong there. These problems keep us from hearing God's word in its full power and clarity, even though they do not cause false prophecy in the sense used above. Besides false prophecy, bad prophecy can be divided into three categories.

Impure Prophecy

Frequently people who prophesy will mix their own thoughts in with the word of the Lord in such a way that God's word is altered or distorted. This happens especially when people are just beginning to exercise the prophetic gift. In one sense, something of our own thought always appears in the prophecies we give, because prophecy operates *through* us. But when our thoughts add to the word of the Lord, or take something away from it, or distort its meaning, the value of our prophecy is greatly diminshed. We cannot rely upon impure prophecy as the Lord's word.

Weak Prophecy

Some prophecy comes across almost like a long distance phone call through a bad connection. The power which accompanies a message from God just isn't there. Weak prophecy is not exactly dangerous, in that it won't lead anyone astray. But it is not much of a help either. The power of the Holy Spirit at work in the prophetic word is important. Without it a prophecy is like an old seed: it may look fine, but there won't be much life in it.

Sloppy Prophecy

Sloppy speech detracts from the word of the Lord. By "sloppy speech," I mean broken and halting sentences, or overly casual and colloquial speech. We do not have to be eloquent to prophesy well—a young child or an uneducated man can speak with clarity and dignity—but we do have to avoid sloppiness. A man who has an appointment with his banker or an interview for a job, will carefully avoid using slang terms or poor grammar. We ought to have the same care for God's word. Sloppy prophecy should not be accepted as "good" prophecy.

The Submission of Prophecy

No prophet is his own authority. Prophecy has to be submitted to the Christian community for judgment. *The prophetic word must be attested to by the community*. That principle is fundamental to the exercise of the prophetic gift. Beware of *any* prophet who will not accept the judgment of others about the word which he speaks. No individual has the ability to determine with full certainty that he has spoken the word of the Lord.

Every one of us, without exception, can be deceived. Our own thoughts, our ambitions, the flattery of others, the lies of Satan—any of these can deceive us. But God will take care to see that his *people* are not finally deceived. We can rely on the judgment of the Christian community to guard us from deception. Of course, a Christian group can also be deceived. Examples of Christian groups or communities which have been led into error are not hard to find. But a group that is functioning well can usually be trusted. If the judgment of a healthy community is not infallible, it is usually reliable.

Every prophet has to be under the authority of others. In practice, this means that every one who prophesies should let the group he belongs to weigh and test the word he speaks, to determine whether it truly comes from God. And every Christian group has to take on the responsibility of testing prophecy.

I know a man who began to prophesy eight years ago. Nothing in his prophecies was seriously wrong at first, but he refused to listen to the correction and judgments other people offered about the things he said. He believed that he had better judgment than anyone else. As time went on, his prophecies became more and more problematic, until he was finally giving prophecies which were actually false. In the end, he prophesied that his son was the messiah.

This man was not "crazy" when he began prophesying; he was actually a good Christian man. But he allowed himself to be very seriously deceived.

The prophetic word is subject to the judgment of the Christian community. And anyone who prophesies should be in a Christian group which will actively work to test out the word he speaks.

Just as the prophet has a responsibility to submit himself and the word which he speaks to the group, so the group has a responsibility to test and judge the prophetic word. The prophet should receive guidance, encouragement, and correction from the group. If he does not, the group will reap the harvest of its neglect. Prophecy will grow either weak and impure or die away entirely if the group does not tend it well.

Every group ought to agree upon some way to share their judgments about prophecy and ensure that advice or correction is given. In most cases, individual members of a group should *not* take it upon themselves to give correction or advice to people who prophesy. Rather, members should share their discernment with the leaders of the group, and the leaders should take on the responsibility of giving feedback and, where necessary, correction to those who prophesy.

So far it may seem that the prophetic word has to be submitted to the Christian community just so people will not be led astray by impure or false prophecy. But even very good prophecy must be submitted to the judgment of the community. It is the place of the prophet to receive and proclaim the word. It is the place of the community to verify that the word comes from God.

Even experienced and reliable prophets can grow in the prophetic gift. No one should decide that he has reached full maturity in any gift: we will always find room for correction and improvement in our service to the Lord. It is right for a prophet who has been tested and proved reliable to have confidence in exercising his gift. But he must remember that *the basis of his own confidence is the confidence which the Christian community has placed in him.*

Mutual Love

A relationship of brotherly love and support between those who exercise prophetic gifts and others in the group is a key to having prophecy work well. A person who is afraid that he will be criticized or harshly corrected for making a mistake will find it difficult to prophesy at all. Those who give impure or weak or sloppy prophecies ought to be corrected, but the correction should be given in a way which will encourage rather than condemn them.

One could correct a prophet by saying, "That was not a very good prophecy." But if that is all the prophet is told, he will not know how to improve. A more helpful correction might be stated: "I think that you should be more relaxed when you speak in prophecy. The prophecy you gave today was very hard to understand, because you spoke too quickly. In the future, try to speak a little more slowly." Such a correction is not only clear and helpful, it communicates support and encouragement as well.

By the same token, those who prophesy have to see their exercise of that gift as a service for others. They should prophesy out of love for their brothers and sisters, not out of desire for attention or glory. Very often you can tell whether a person is sincerely acting out of love by the way he responds to correction. Those who prophesy in order to serve will accept and even desire correction, because correction will help them serve better in the future. But often people are hurt or angered by correction because they are prophesying for themselves—for their own pleasure or reputation or status—rather than for others.

Testing Prophecy

God has provided abundant wisdom for testing and judging prophetic utterance. There are four areas of judgment in testing out prophetic words, and I will describe each of them in detail.

The Life of the Prophet

For no good tree bears bad fruit, nor again does a bad tree bear good fruit, for each tree is known by its own fruit. Figs are not gathered from thorns, nor grapes picked from a bramble bush.

(Luke 6:43-44)

The first and most fundamental test of a prophetic utterance is the life of the person who gives it. If he leads a life worthy of God and manifests the fruit of the Holy Spirit, he can be trusted. If his life is not that of a Christian, or if his Christian life is very immature or inconsistent, he should not be trusted.

Jesus' principle that a tree can be known by its fruits extends to every area of the Christian life. In the scriptural lists of the qualities required in the elder or bishop of a Christian community, only one "spiritual gift" is mentioned (1 Tim. 3:1-7, Tit. 1:5-9). What counts, in other words, is not spiritual experiences or extraordinary gifts, but the way a person lives (cf., pp. 63-66).

The gifts of the Holy Spirit are not merit badges handed out to those who excel in virtue, they are equipment given for the service of God. Men are not holy because they exercise spiritual gifts, nor do they exercise spiritual gifts because they are holy. Oftentimes we see people who are very young in the Christian life given gifts for service which their older and more mature brothers do not have. But there is a connection between the holiness of a person's life and the gifts which he exercises. The more mature, stable, and virtuous a person is, the more we can rely upon him to exercise the gifts of the Spirit with purity and power.

"Unknown prophets" should be avoided. Many people can come and speak a very spiritual sounding message, while their own lives are less than a shining example of Christianity. We should be assured that those who speak God's word to us in prophecy are living godly lives. Now this does not mean that we cannot hear and accept a prophetic word spoken by someone who is immature as a Christian. One of the most powerful prophecies which I have ever heard was spoken by a man who was young in the life of the Holy Spirit. It does mean, however, that we should more carefully test the words such people speak.

Let's say that you are looking for a contractor to build a house for you. You would naturally look for a man with a solid reputation for honesty and good work. Someone who had been in the business for thirty years and was well known as a dependable builder would probably be your first choice. You *could* hire a contractor who was just getting started; he might even do a better job than the well known man. But if you were to hire a new man, you would undoubtedly be careful to check his credentials and keep an eye on his work. That only makes sense. And you would probably not hire any man who had a bad reputation as a contractor. After all, why should you entrust such an important job to a man who is known to be unworthy of trust?

This simple common sense applies to all spiritual gifts, and in a special way to prophets. We can be easily impressed by men who speak eloquently and "profoundly." But the test of whether someone is truly spiritual is not the sound of his prophecy; it is the quality and character of his Christian life.

Tests of the Message

The second area to test in judging prophecies is the actual content of the message. Is it in line with Christian teaching? Paul told the people of Galatia that if he himself, or even an angel should preach to them a different gospel than that which he had preached, he or the angel should be cursed (Gal. 1:8-9). Nothing which contradicts Christian teaching can be admitted as true prophecy. We have several guidelines to help us judge whether the content of a message is true or false.

The first guide is *Scripture*. We know that Scripture is the rule against which all other truths must be tested. Anything which contradicts Scripture is false. If someone should prophesy that Jesus did not rise from the dead, to take one example, we would know that the prophecy was false. Paul says that if Christ did not rise from the dead then the whole Christian life if futile (1 Cor. 15:13-19).

A second test of the prophetic message is *the body of teaching central to all of Christian life*. In times past this body of teaching has often been known as "the rule of faith" or "creed." Several compact statements of these teachings exist which can serve as simple "rules of faith;" The Nicene Creed is one example. Anything given in prophetic form which is not consistent with the main body of Christian teaching must be rejected as false.

There is a significant difficulty in applying this criterion: Christians don't all agree on what is true Christian teaching.

There has to be some authority outside the individual Christian community, some guide to what is or is not Christian teaching. I cannot attempt here a full discussion of how true "Christian teaching" can be known. As a Roman Catholic, I believe that the authority for identifying what is true and essential Christian truth (and therefore what can be accepted in prophecy) rests with the teaching authority of the Catholic Church. Others, who are not Catholic, will approach this question in a different way. Beyond that fundamental difference, there are many questions about Christian truth which are not settled even by the teaching authority of the Catholic Church. Many questions have not been authoritatively defined by the Church. Catholics can legitimately differ on many points as to what constitutes true Christian teaching.

This difficulty, however, is not caused by *prophecy*. It is a difficulty caused by the condition of Christianity today. It hampers us in our attempts to judge prophecy; but it hampers us also in our attempts to discern teaching and preaching generally.

My own experience has been that such problems only rarely prove to be a serious obstacle in judging prophecy. If a Christian group is in good order, and if the members of the group are sensitive and mature in their exercise of prophecy, difficulties over basic Christian teaching seldom arise.

These first two guidelines will help us when a prophetic message is clearly false; it will alert us to anything which is contrary to Christian truth. But we will probably not hear many prophecies which go against clear Christian truth. (I have heard maybe two or three in the last eight years.) There are, however, prophetic messages which do not contradict Christianity, but still seem questionable.

Five years ago at a meeting of our community someone spoke out a prophecy that just didn't sit right with most of those who were present. The message was not obviously wrong, but it wasn't right either. The message sounded very important, but it also sound a little mysterious. I feel confident that the prophecy was not so much a word from the Lord as it was a product of the imagination of the man who gave it. Some people become fascinated with very "spiritual" things, and usually "spiritual" in this sense means "unreal." The man who gave this prophecy had given several others just like it. None of them had any understandable connection with real life. He thought they were "spiritual."

Most of the time, we should be able to understand the prophecies which we receive. Every now and then the Lord will speak in prophecy, and we will not understand the message right away. When that happens, we should simply keep in mind what God has spoken, and he will make it clear at the appropriate time. If someone regularly gives prophecies which are hard to understand, it probably indicates that he has a problem rather than a spiritual gift.

Testing the Spirits

In order to determine that something is a direct prophetic word, we have to "test the spirit" of the prophecy. Testing the message of a prophetic utterance cannot normally tell us whether the message is really from God. It can tell us that the message is definitely *not* from God—that it violates Scripture or Christian teaching—but that is all. I could "prophesy" at anytime that God wants you to serve him. If I had just decided to say that in prophetic form, it would not really be a prophecy. But simply testing the message could not tell you that. It would tell you that the message itself is true, but it could not tell you whether the message was really a prophecy.

When I say "test the spirit" I mean just that: test and see what spirit is behind the prophetic utterance. True prophecy comes from the Holy Spirit, and we can determine whether the Holy Spirit has inspired something or not. Every Christian is in a relationship with the Lord which allows him to know the Lord's voice.

The one who enters through the gate is the shepherd of the sheep; the keeper opens the gate for him. The sheep hear his voice as he calls his own by name and leads them out. When he has brought out all those that are his, he walks in front of them, and the sheep follow him because they recognize his voice. They will not follow a stranger; such a one they will flee, because they do not recognize a stranger's voice.

(John 10:2-5)

We can recognize the voice of the Lord. Each of us has received the same Holy Spirit who speaks in prophecy. When a true prophecy is spoken, our spirits will respond; we will know that we have heard the Lord. When we hear a voice other than the Lord's, we will recognize it as the voice of a stranger.

There is a simple physical principle termed "resonance." Objects have certain characteristic frequencies at which they vibrate. If you cause one object (for instance a bell) to vibrate near another object with the same characteristic frequency (another bell of the same size and weight and shape), the second object will begin to vibrate by itself. That is something like what happens when we hear the voice of the Lord—we resonate.

So the first test of whether or not something comes from the Holy Spirit is simply *the response in our own heart and spirit*. If we feel in our hearts a peaceful assurance that we are listening to the same Spirit who gives us life in the Lord, we can have some confidence that the prophecy is from the Lord. If the spiritual nature of the prophecy disturbs or repels us, we should not place confidence in it.

There is an important qualification on this principle. Many times individuals will not feel any real spiritual response to prophecy—either positive or negative. That is normal. It does not necessarily indicate that the prophecy is not valid, nor does it indicate that there is something wrong with the listeners. The point of the principle is that many people do experience some "spiritual response" to prophecy. That response, though not definitive in itself, can help us determine whether a prophecy is from the Lord.

The second way to test the spirit of a prophecy is to judge *its spiritual tone and effect.* Prophecy which is frightening, harsh, condemning or critical seldom comes from the Holy Spirit. The Lord will often use prophecy to correct us and call us to repentance; sometimes he will even point out specific areas in our lives which are not right. But when God speaks to us, he does not condemn. Instead, he calls us to return to him, that he may forgive us and change us.

Occasionally someone will decide that his personal criticisms of his church or of some other person will carry more weight if given as prophecy. When that happens, we may hear a prophecy in which the Lord seems to exactly agree with the person prophesying! I knew of a group several years ago which had difficulty because one member was giving prophecies which criticized and belittled the leadership of the group. Not surprisingly, the person who gave those prophecies was resentful and bitter toward the leaders of the group.

The Lord speaks to us as a loving father: sometimes stern, sometimes pleased, sometimes warning us to change. But he always speaks out of love; if he corrects or disciplines us, he accompanies that correction with an assurance of his love and an encouragement to change. No true prophecy will reveal a God who is vindictive or cruel or harsh or critical.

These "tests of the spirit" have to be qualified. Any one person may find a particular prophecy either very pleasing or very disturbing, not because of the spiritual nature of the prophecy, but because of his personal thoughts, problems or preferences. For instance, David could have found Nathan's prophetic description of his sins extremely disturbing (2 Sam.

12). Had David been unwilling to repent, he probably would have been repulsed by the prophecy rather than moved to remorse. The problem would not have been in the spirit of the prophecy, but in the condition of David's life.

Because of the weakness we all experience in our humanity, we have to rely not only upon our own judgment, but also on the judgment of others. The fact that we feel elated or repelled by a particular prophecy is only one piece of evidence that must be considered along with the evidence of others.

The third test of the spirit in prophecy is *whether or not the prophetic utterance glorifies the Lord Jesus*. We may not always be able to tell whether a *particular* prophecy glorified the Lord or not, but if over a period of time we notice that the prophecies which a certain person gives or the prophecies we hear in a certain group do not lead us to acknowledge and worship the Lord, then something is wrong.

Finally, some people have been given *a special gift of discernment,* of "distinguishing between spirits" (1 Cor. 12:10). Those who have received such a gift will be able to tell with a greater clarity and swiftness when some spirit other than the Lord's is at work in prophecy.

Does It Come to Pass?

In the book of Deuteronomy, there is a warning to avoid as false any prophet who prophesies something which does not actually come to pass:

> And if you say in your heart, "How may we know the word which the Lord has not spoken?"—when a prophet speaks in the name of the Lord, if the word does not come to pass or come true, that is a word which the Lord has not spoken; the prophet has spoken it presumptuously, and you need not be afraid of him.
>
> (Deut. 18:21-22)

In other words, if a prophecy predicts that a particular event will happen, and it does not, then the word was not from the Lord. There are two qualifications on this rule. The first is given a little earlier in Deuteronomy:

> And if a prophet arises among you or a dreamer of dreams, and gives you a sign or a wonder, and the sign or wonder which he tells you comes to pass, and if he says, "let us go after other gods," which you have not known, "and let us serve them," you shall not listen to the words of that prophet or that dreamer of dreams; for the Lord your God is testing you, to know whether you love the Lord your God with all your heart and all your soul.
>
> (Deut. 13:1-3)

False prophets can arise and make predictions which come true. So even if what the prophet predicts "comes to pass," he may not be a true prophet.

The second qualification is that many times when the Lord speaks something in a predictive way, there is an "if" attached to it. The prophecy may say, "*If* you are faithful, such-and-such will happen" or "*if* you repent, I will bless you." Something which is predicted in prophecy may not come to pass because we are not faithful to the conditions that the Lord gives us.

Even so, the rule is important. When a prophetic message is given which predicts that something will happen, we should watch to see whether that word was true. If what was predicted comes to pass, our faith and confidence in the word of the Lord will be built up. If the word was not true, we should do something to see that such mistaken prophetic utterances do not contine.

Does It Bear Fruit?

A true word from the Lord will bring forth good fruit—good results—among the people who hear it. Most of the prophecies which we receive will not be predictions, but all of them will have effects. If we pay attention to the effect that prophetic utterances have, we can judge their worth. A word from the Lord will produce life, peace, hope, love, and all the other fruit of the Holy Spirit. A word which is not from the Lord will either produce the fruit of evil—strife, anger, jealousy, lust, indifference—or it will have no effect at all.

We probably will not be able to judge the fruit of every single prophetic message, but we can look for the overall effects of the prophecies we are receiving. If we notice that every time a particular person prophesies he causes lack of peace or some other bad effect, we can judge that something is wrong with his prophesying.

Two or three years ago in our community people began to sing out prophetic songs when we were worshipping together. We were not then familiar with prophetic song, and some of us tended to wonder if they were really inspired. It was not possible to tell by looking at the effects produced by any one prophetic song, but over a period of weeks we noticed that everytime someone sang out a prophecy a deep spirit of worship came upon the group. With time, the whole way in which we prayed together deepened and improved. We could then see that this type of prophetic song bore fruit which was from the Holy Spirit.

Once again, the condition of those who receive a prophecy can affect its ability to produce fruit. Jeremiah's prophecies caused strife, anger, and violence, but that was because those who heard them were not willing to accept God's word. Nothing can replace our constant and pure-hearted desire to follow the Lord and receive his word. For a community or group which is not in good spiritual condition, no test of prophecy will suffice.

Growing in Judgment

The guidelines for judging prophecy which I have given

above are not a set of special rules which, when carefully applied, produce an automatic answer from the Lord. They are only *guidelines;* they can help us make a judgment about prophetic utterances, but *we* have to make the judgment. Two or three of these guidelines can help us determine that something is definitely *not* from the Lord (the tests of the message especially), but none of them can tell us with certainty that something *is* from the Lord. We have to decide that.

Our judgment will mature and deepen as we grow in the life of the Holy Spirit, and as we gain experience in testing prophecy. We could compare it to growing in judgment about art. An art expert can tell you that a particular painting is very good for this or that reason, that another painting is good, but not extraordinarily good because it lacks a certain texture, and so on. When he makes these judgments about a painting, he does not sit down with a list of rules and check them off one by one. He has learned to keep those rules in mind whenever he looks at art. He does not have to look at the rules closely because they have become a part of the way he sees things.

Now let's say that you ask this art expert to teach you good judgment about art. He would probably begin by telling you a number of rules or guidelines for determining whether something is good. Then you would take a painting and carefully go over it, applying the rules he had given you. When finished, you probably wouldn't feel very confident about your judgment. If the expert disagreed with your judgment, I doubt that you'd argue with him, even though you had followed all the rules in forming your opinion. That's because the rules in themselves can't tell you what is good or bad; they are only guidelines which can help you decide what *you* say.

After working over the guidelines for a long time and looking at very many paintings, you will finally gain real confidence in your ability to judge art all on your own. But when you reach that point, you won't be using the guidelines in quite the same way. They will have become part of the way you see art, not something you have to make a conscious effort to apply.

Growing in discernment about prophecy works the same way. At first we have to apply quite carefully the various guidelines to make a judgment. And even when we have applied them, we will not be too sure of our judgment. As we grow in experience, the guidelines will take a different place, and our judgment will be confident and sure. At all times, especially when we are inexperienced, we have to rely heavily on the judgment of others. If you hear a prophecy and are not sure what to think of it—ask someone else, particularly someone whose judgment you trust, what he thought of it. We will always need the judgment of others to have certainty that we have heard the Lord. Yet we can come to have real confidence in our individual judgment too. We can have assurance that if Jeremiah and Hananiah held their "prophetic duel" before us, we would choose the man who truly spoke from God.

Chapter Eight

Growing in Prophetic Service

Most Christians would be horrified if anyone told them to become spiritually ambitious. Actually desiring to give prophecies or work miracles or even lead prayer meetings seems inconsistent with the humility expected of a Christian. And in fact, the desire to experience these gifts can be coupled with an unchristian ambition for personal renown or position. Yet that is not to say that all spiritual ambition is wrong. We can seek to experience the workings of the Holy Spirit not for selfish motives but because of our love for other Christians.

When Paul wrote his first letter to the Corinthians, he was apparently concerned that they were misusing the gifts of the Spirit. However, he did not tell them to stop using the gifts. He gave thanks that they had received God's power in such abundance, and he urged them to continue seeking the operations of the Holy Spirit—"especially that you might prophesy" (1 Cor. 14:1). But he also pointed out that those gifts would mean nothing unless they were exercised in love. His entire discussion of spiritual gifts centers on a profound meditation on Christian love (1 Cor. 13).

If Christians are serving one another with true and godly love, their desire to receive the gifts of the Holy Spirit will take its rightful place. God gives his gifts to each individual Christian so that the whole body of Christ may be complete and fully equipped. We ought each to long to take the place in Christ's body that the Lord has assigned to us (cf., 1 Tim. 3:1), and we ought to hunger for the gifts and workings of the Spirit which will enable us to take that place.

The attitude which should characterize our use of the spiritual gifts is expressed clearly in a passage from **Paul's** letter to the Philippians.

> So if there is any encouragement in Christ, any incentive of love, any participation in the Spirit, any affection and sympathy, complete my joy by being of the same mind, having the same love, being of full accord and of one mind. Do nothing from selfishness and conceit, but in humility count others better than yourselves. Let each of you look not only to his own interests but also to the interests of others. Have this mind among yourselves which you have in Christ Jesus, who, though he was in the form of God, did not count equality with God a thing to be grasped, but emptied himself, taking the form of a servant, being born in the likeness of men. And being found in human form he humbled himself and became obedient unto death, even death on a cross. Therefore God has highly exalted him and bestowed on him the name which is above every name, that at the name of Jesus every knee should bow, in heaven and on earth and under the earth, and every tongue confess that Jesus Christ is Lord, to the glory of God the father.
>
> (Phil. 2:1-11)

Jesus is our model, and it is after his example that we pattern our own Christian lives. If Jesus had the attitude of a servant (the word for servant used here can also be translated *slave*), we should take on the attitude of a servant. This passage points out two attitudes contrary to true servanthood. The first is "selfishness." The word translated here as "selfishness" is a Greek word which means "seeking a position." The word was used in Paul's time to describe someone seeking a political office. Non-Christian Greeks would not have found this phrase negative or insulting; it simply described what politicians were doing. But when Paul used it, he gave it a negative meaning, because "seeking a place for yourself" is contrary to being concerned for the interests of others. The second attitude that Paul condemned is "conceit" or "vainglory." Vainglory is the glory which men give; true glory comes from God. If we are seeking glory from men, then we are not seeking glory from God. Neither are we serving our brothers and sisters.

If we pattern ourselves after Jesus, we cannot live for ourselves and our interests, but for God and God's people and for their interests. To become like Jesus, we must put aside selfish ambition and take on an ambition to serve. If a true ambition to serve our brothers and sisters leads us to desire the gifts of the Holy Spirit, our ambition is holy. If ambition for our own status or reputation leads us to seek those gifts, we stand condemned and will be unable to help the people of God.

The more fully we are blessed with the workings of the Spirit, the better our service will be. Anyone who prophesies ought to desire to prophesy with more power, fulness and depth, because he will then be a more useful servant.

Here we must make a distinction between two ways of desiring to prophesy. All Christians should desire to prophesy on occasion, as Paul tells us: "Earnestly desire the spiritual gifts, especially that you might prophesy" (1 Cor. 14:1). Prophecy "builds up" the body of Christ. It is a useful and practical gift. If a brother or sister is sick, we should desire to have God work to heal them. In the same way, when the community gathers together before the Lord, we should desire to hear God speak to us. Our desire to prophesy is right and good if it is focused on meeting the needs of the Lord's people.

But at the same time, we should not desire to be a prophet, unless *we know* God has called us to that (cf., p. 48).

Something has gone wrong if our desire is focused on *being something* among God's people—being a prophet, or being a healer, etc. If we do know that God has made us a prophet, if he has assigned us that place in the body, then we ought to desire to serve in that place as fully as we can. A desire to be a prophet should come *after* we have learned that God has given us that place in the body. Our will in that regard should conform itself to God's will.

In practice, this simply means that we should prophesy to whatever extent God gives us the ability to prophesy, neither holding back a gift we have received, nor reaching out to grasp something that God has not given.

Desiring to prophesy in a way that will serve God and serve our brothers and sisters has some practical consequences. We will soon have opportunities to discover what our attitudes truly are. When we are offered correction about the way we prophesy, how do we respond? If we are hurt or upset, we show that we feel more concern for our own interests than for serving God. Anyone who honestly desires to serve will be hungry for correction, because correction will teach him to serve in a better way. If someone else in the group begins to prophesy more frequently or more powerfully than we do, what is our reaction? If we become unhappy or jealous, we show that our true desire is to earn ourselves a reputation or attract other people's attention. Anyone who honestly wants to serve God's people by helping them hear God's word will rejoice when that word is spoken, no matter who does the speaking.

Becoming a servant after the model of Jesus is the root and the ground, the beginning, the middle, and the end of the prophetic gift. We need a servant's attitude in order to begin prophesying; we need it to improve our exercise of the gift. Several other attitudes which we will examine in this chapter can also help us grow in the gift of prophecy, but the attitude of the servant is most fundamental. Without it, we have nothing.

> And if I have prophetic powers, and understand all mysteries and all knowledge . . . but have not love, I am nothing. . . . Love never ends; as for prophecies, they will pass away . . . For our knowledge is imperfect and our prophecy is imperfect . . . Faith, hope and love abide, these three; but the greatest of these is love.
>
> (1 Cor. 13:2, 8-9, 13)

Prophecy and Inspiration

We cannot just decide on our own to prophesy more frequently or more powerfully or to receive more revelation. The prophetic gift depends completely upon the inspiration of the Holy Spirit. So, to a great extent, growing in prophecy amounts to waiting on the Lord. Perhaps for two years you have given prophecies regularly, but they have all been relatively short and not very powerful. Now you are eager for that gift to develop. You would like to break out in prophetic song or to deliver a truly powerful and life-changing prophecy or to receive a revelation from the Lord that provides direct guidance for some difficult situation. But as you wait week after week for these things to happen, your prophecies remain the same—short and not very powerful.

Well, you do have to wait. You cannot sing inspired songs just because you want to. But you can wait in a way which allows you to receive more from the Lord. You can wait with eagerness to have the Lord do more through you. You can tell the Lord in prayer that you are willing to serve him fully and that you want to prophesy more fully. You can look for the

Lord to inspire you in new ways, so that you will be able to perceive his inspiration when it does come.

And you can pray. Seek God daily—not just for the sake of prophecy, but for his own sake. We cannot receive any gift from the Lord if we are not abiding with him in a deep and intimate personal relationship. Spend time just getting to know the Lord and learning to love him, but also seeking him for his word. Ask him to reveal his word to his people, and tell him that you want to hear that word. At times when you or people you know especially need to hear God's word, go to him earnestly for it. When the elders in Jerusalem asked Jeremiah for the word of the Lord (Jer. 42), the prophet had to go off for ten days seeking the face of God before he received it.

It often helps to talk and pray with others who prophesy. Sharing with others the experiences and difficulties you have had will allow you to learn from them. As you pray together, God can speak to you about serving him through the prophetic gift. These gatherings can also provide simple encouragement for people who prophesy. Our community has held such a meeting every other week for the past two years with very good results. Even though apparently "nothing" happens at any given meeting, overall the meeting has improved and strengthened the exercise of the prophetic gift in the life of the community.

At some of these meetings we simply pray. We pray for one another; we pray that the Lord will speak to the community powerfully; we pray that sins or bad attitudes which hamper our service might be removed. At other times we share our experience and exercise of the prophetic gift with one another, asking for advice or help with difficulties we have encountered. On other occasions we listen to tapes or read pamphlets about prophecy and discuss them together.

The community's practice has been to invite anyone who experiences prophecy to attend these meetings. Some of those present have been prophesying for many years. Others have been prophesying for only a few months, or even a few weeks. The mutual support, encouragement, and teaching help everyone who attends.

Faith

Prophecy is received and given by faith. No one can speak in prophecy unless he has faith that God has inspired his words and will uphold them through the action of his Holy Spirit. With some prophecies in particular (for instance predictive prophecies) we need faith simply to proclaim what we receive.

We can easily slip into thinking that prophecy depends upon us, rather than upon the Holy Spirit. I have known some people to grow so tense and nervous that they could not prophesy at all because they were relying on themselves and not on the Lord. One woman had a very clear and strong gift of prophecy, but finally stopped prophesying because she was afraid that she couldn't. In every prayer meeting, she would think, "I have a gift of prophecy, and I am supposed to use it. I had better get something to happen!" But then she would find that nothing happened.

There is a real difference between "stirring up the gift" and "prophesying by our own power." The latter cannot be done. To "stir up the gift" means to put ourselves in readiness to *receive* a prophecy from God. "Prophesying by our own power" means we are trying to work up a prophecy ourselves rather than waiting to receive it from the Lord. An experience I had two years ago illustrates the difference.

An important meeting of our community was coming up and I knew that we would need to hear the Lord speak very clearly. I started trying to get myself ready to prophesy. But I tried in the wrong way: I began to pressure myself to have a prophecy for that meeting. By the time the meeting finally came, I had made myself extremely tense and anxious. I sat through the first half hour desperately trying to get something to say. Then I realized my mistake; I didn't *have* to prophesy, I only had to speak a word if God gave me a word to speak. Immediately I relaxed and looked to the Lord peacefully. And in fact, the Lord did have a word to speak. I was able to receive it from him and prophesy.

Peter had the same experience when Jesus asked him to walk on the water. Obviously Peter couldn't walk on the water, but he stepped out of the boat in response to the Lord's invitation. He wasn't trying to walk on water; he was just doing what the Lord asked him to do. But when he became frightened, he did try to walk on the water, and he sank. As soon as he moved from simply responding in faith to the Lord to trying to do something himself, he failed We will too.

This principle applies even more when we want to grow in the exercise of prophecy. If we cannot prophesy even on a simple level through our own efforts, how much less can we grow in the gift by our own effort! Jesus said that none of us, by being anxious to do it, can add anything to the length of our life. But by faith in God we will receive full care from our Father in heaven. In the same way, we cannot add any growth to our service of God through prophecy by being anxious about it. But by faith we can receive the utter fulness of that gift.

Submissiveness

To become stronger and purer in prophecy we must also be submissive. Being submissive simply means taking the place that God assigns to us and acting in a way appropriate to that place. We must learn to be submissive to God and submissive to the Christian community.

First of all, we must be submissive to God. Perhaps God wants to give us an exceptionally powerful prophetic gift. Perhaps he does not. Whatever he wants to do, we should accept his plan joyfully. For two years after I first spoke in prophecy I exercised the gift very frequently. And then, suddenly, it seemed to stop: during one whole year I scarcely prophesied at all. That year produced some turmoil within me. Here I had thought that God wanted to make me a prophet, and suddenly the gift was just leaving! I discovered that I wasn't quite as willing to take the place God assigned to me as I thought I was. I was happy to obey the Lord so long as I knew that he wanted to make me a prophet, but not so sure about obeying him when prophecy didn't seem to be involved. That year taught me that I had to change my attitude about serving the Lord. I had to learn to be happy and peaceful in whatever service God called me to. If he wanted me to be a half-time prophet, then I would be a half-time prophet joyfully.

We must find our joy in God's will, not in our own. If we want to prophesy, yet God assigns us a different service among his people, we should accept the service he gives us and forget about becoming a prophet. If, like Jeremiah, we do not want to prophesy and yet God calls us to that, we have to lay down our will and take up the prophetic service.

We must also be submissive to God in the way we prophesy. Maybe our greatest delight is to sing inspired and prophetic songs. But if the people we are serving don't need inspired songs, we should not sing them. Perhaps we would like to prophesy before large groups of people. Yet if God wants us to prophesy only in small groups, it should become our joy to prophesy in small groups. A servant is not supposed to do what he likes to do, but what his master gives him to do. The good servant is one who takes care to do just what his master instructs him—neither more nor less.

The day may come when the Lord wants us to take initiative in exercising the gift he has given to his body through us. If it does, then we should vigorously carry out his will. We should neither anticipate that day nor hold back from it.

The second way we must be submissive is to be submissive to the body of Christ. Often the way that the Lord makes his will known to us is through the instructions we receive from the Christians we are serving. We must be submissive to those instructions just as we must be submissive to the Lord. I have at times asked certain people in our community not to prophesy in public meetings for some period of time, either because they needed to grow and improve in the gift or because their prophecy was not beneficial to the community. I have also corrected people in the way that they prophesied. All of these instructions have helped prophecy grow in our community. Similiar instructions may be given to anyone of us at some time: if they are, we should submit to them, knowing that they are given for the good of the Christian people.

In the meetings of our community we have established an order for the exercise of the prophetic gift. Normally people have to ask the leader of the meeting if they may prophesy. That order is necessary because a very large number of people attend our meetings (usually over a thousand). At first we resisted the idea of establishing this order, because we thought it might stifle the freedom of the meetings. We have found, however, that just the opposite has happened. The exercise of prophecy has flourished because the regulation of the gift is appropriate to the situation. In a different setting such regulation *could* stifle the Spirit, and some day in new circumstances we may change the approach we are using. But for the time being, it is a great help.

It is the place of the prophet to be obedient to the leaders of his group. At times the Lord may correct or admonish those leaders through the prophet, but still he must be submissive to the leaders, trusting in God to work through them. In this way, the prophetic gift can be properly regulated.

Patience

You will not become another Isaiah overnight or even in the next five years. God has to work a great many changes in all of us before we reach maturity in his service. And we need patience in order for those gifts he has given to come to their maturity.

Patience, according to Scripture, is the ability to faithfully and peacefully keep at something over a long period of time. The word carries with it the notion of determination. Our realization that maturity will only come with time (and probably only with a long time) should not prompt us to just sit back and not expect much change or improvement. Instead, we should persevere in our determination to grow, not being discouraged if things don't seem to change quickly. If God has called us to serve him through prophecy, then he will supply every working of the Spirit, every quality of character, every grace necessary for us. Be patient. Thank God for every grace and improvement; hope in God for the changes which still have to come; believe in God because he is faithful.

Prophecy in the Church Today

The gift of prophecy is being rediscovered and revitalized today among Christians. At present, this rediscovery is occurring in the context of the charismatic renewal. Perhaps a million Christians have been brought into an awareness of the reality of God's power through the gifts of the Holy Spirit in the last fifteen years. But God does not intend that his gifts be experienced by only a few. One million Christians is roughly one-tenth of one per cent of the Christians in the world today. If God's power is to be unleashed in its fullness, over nine hundred and ninety million Christians will have to experience for themselves the "charismatic" workings of the Holy Spirit. Until we see prophecy and miracles and discernment of spirits and all of the other gifts of the Spirit actively employed by all of God's people, we are short of God's purpose. In May of 1975 I witnessed a striking event in modern Christian history. At a mass in St. Peter's Basilica in Rome, the "charismatic" gifts, including the gift of prophecy, were freely exercised. I was struck by the complete appropriateness of that service. Surely it should be the normal experience of the church.

The gift of prophecy is not essential to salvation. The kingdom of God could increase (and has increased) in the absence of prophetic manifestations. Yet, to decide that we will do without prophecy just because it is possible to do without prophecy is to settle for less, just because we *can* settle for less. A group of Roman Catholic theologians and pastoral leaders has recently described the weakness of a "settle for less" approach:

> . . . By the way of example, imagine for a moment that the full spectrum of how the Spirit comes to visibility in a charism extends from A to Z. . . . Here it is supposed that in the section of the spectrum which extends from A to P are such charisms as generosity in giving alms and other acts of mercy (Rom. 12:8) and teaching activities of various kinds. Obviously, the charisms in the A to P section of the spectrum are so numerous and varied as to be beyond the possiblity of numbering and naming them. The section of the spectrum which extends from P to Z is supposed here to include such charisms as prophecy, gifts of healing, working of miracles, tongues, interpretation.
>
> It is evident that in the life of the early Church the communities expected that the Spirit would manifest himself in ministries and services which might fall within the spectrum which extends from A to P, but they also expected the Spirit to manifest himself in the other ministries and services within the section of the spectrum which extends from P to Z. They were aware that prophecy, gifts of healing, working of miracles, tongues and interpretation were real charisms, real possibilities for the life of the church. . . . In this they differ from most contemporary communities. Communities in the Church today are not aware that the charisms in the section of the spectrum which extends from P to Z are possibilities for the life of the Church . . .
>
> For a community to have a limited expectation as to how the Spirit will manifest himself in its midst can pro-

foundly affect the life and experience of that community
. . . . This is obvious when one recalls that the charisms are
ministries to the church and to the world. And if a community limits how the Spirit manifests himself there is
some measure of impoverishment in the total life of that
local church.[1]

Certainly we do not *have to have* the gift of prophecy operating in the church. But if God offers the gift, if the gift will
increase our effectiveness in serving God and our neighbor,
then it is *wrong* to decline it.

There are, generally speaking, two reasons for the lack of
prophetic activity among Christians today. The first reason is
described above: a lack of "awareness" that these gifts are
real possibilities in the church today, and a consequent "limited expectation" that these gifts will operate. The second
reason is fear—fear that prophecy will be misused.

God himself is taking care of the first difficulty. He is making us aware of the real possibility of receiving and exercising
the prophetic gifts, by giving prophetic gifts to Christians.
Prophecy has always been present in the church (see Appendix 1) but the presence of the prophetic gifts over the past
several centuries has not been common enough to help us to
actually expect them. We have been led to think that such gifts
are given only to "special people," or only in rare and extraordinary situations. Today, however, we can see hundreds of
thousands of Christians who have experienced for themselves
the real possibility of receiving prophecy.

Overcoming the second difficulty, fear of misuse of
prophecy, will have to be our responsibility. From one point of
view, we have reasons for our fears. Prophecy can be misused,
and obviously has been misused in the past. But from another
point of view, that fear is evidence of a lack of faith in God.
"What man among you, if his son asks him for bread will give
him a stone? Or if he asks for a fish will give him a serpent? If

you then, who are evil, know how to give good gifts to your children, how much more will your father who is in heaven give good gifts to those who ask him!'' (Matt. 7:9-11). Do we believe that God would offer us a gift which will harm us?

Expecting and receiving prophecy in the church will demand some changes. In an early chapter of this book I described the kind of community life and pastoral authority which is needed to supervise and support the operation of prophecy. That kind of pastoral care does not characterize the church today. In some ways, the church today is not ''in shape'' to handle prophetic gifts. If we are to meet the challenge of a renewed and vital charismatic activity in the church, we will have to examine and in many cases change our pastoral structures. Charismatic gifts are not the fullness of church renewal, but they can serve as a stimulus to a much broader and deeper renewal.

The situation we face in receiving full charismatic activity can be compared to adding a bathroom to a house. At first, the project might seem limited. All that one has to do is build a small addition and install the plumbing. But in the process, we may discover that the current plumbing will be inadequate to handle a new bathroom. Further inspection might reveal that the electrical wiring is not up to the task of supplying power to the outlets and light fixtures in the new room. The installation of a new bathroom could lead to a major change which will affect the whole house.

I personally believe that the pastoral structures of most churches are not adequate to supervise prophetic activity. In most churches, the pastoral work is done by a few selected and specially trained people—the priests and ministers—with perhaps a few lay assistants added to handle certain areas. These specialized pastoral leaders are often so loaded down with administrative tasks that they cannot provide sufficient pastoral care for those under their charge. Furthermore, in virtually every major Christian church, the pastoral leaders move from one congregation to another every several years. This constant reassignment severely limits a pastor's ability to know the people he is caring for. In most cases a personal knowledge of the local church's members is necessary to the discernment and support of prophecy. The current pastoral approach of most churches cuts across this principle.

The Christian people today face a challenge of such magnitude that a serious look at the structures and forms of church life is essential. We need every gift and every working of the Holy Spirit. If we are not prepared to receive these gifts, then we ought to take whatever steps we can to make ourselves ready.

Christianity is emphatically not in a period of growth and expansion. Our era has been described as "post-Christian," and that view is probably realistic. The following opinions, expressed recently by Catholic bishops, probably represent the perception of many leaders in many denominations:

> The difficulties of organized religion express themselves in such ways as declining membership, declining church attendance, and declining contributions. To be sure, a "church" is not constituted by entries in a ledger Nevertheless, the statistics point to basic problems. The churches themselves are in some cases experiencing a crisis of self identity.[2]

> . . . In Italy one can note a rapid process of secularization, or perhaps of "secularism": on the one hand, manifestations of some traditional Christian values are still alive although they can also be the ferment of a new situation; on the other hand, religious practice is declining, the people's thinking is changing while practical and even ideological or cultural materialism is spreading.[3]

Difficulties, fear and doubts arise largely from the fact

that the secularization process is taking place in a Europe
which is "Christian" or "post-Christian" as they say;
i.e., in areas where there are still vestiges of the
Gospel. . . . The evangelization of Europe is in danger of
going ahead under the sign of an almost watered-down
Christianity. . . . [4]

The condition of society today presents a tremendous challenge to anyone who would seek to fulfill the Christian mission. The world around the Christian community is changing, and powerful forces are at work which oppose the proclamation of the Gospel.

The only adequate response is a Christianity which visibly demonstrates and relies upon the power of God, a church which fulfills its prophetic role.[5] The operation of the prophetic gifts is only one aspect of the renewal in spiritual power which we so desperately need, but it is an important aspect. In the first century, God spoke through the prophets to the Christian churches, giving them warning, guidance and direction. Today, God desires to speak directly and clearly to the Christian churches, warning them, building them, and giving them direction. Can we afford not to listen? Can we afford to reject any gift which God gives us now?

The following prophecy was given in the twentieth century:

Behold, I stretch out my hand and catch hold of my people, turning them aside from their own ways and into the way I have chosen.

Behold, today I reach out my hand to form and shape, to mold and fashion my church.

My people are not ready. I gird myself up and march to war, and my people do not march with me. I sound a battle cry and my people hear nothing.

But now I will reach down and shake them. Now I will rouse them from their sleep.

No longer will I wait while my name is held in dishonor. No longer will I hold back while my people are deceived.
I will reveal to this world the immensity of my glory, the power of my love, the strength of my arm.

My people, open your ears and hear me. I have taken hold of you to change you, to force you into my way.

Notes

1. *Theological and Pastoral Orientations on the Catholic Charismatic Renewal* (Ann Arbor, Michigan: Word of Life 1974) pp. 17-18.

2. *A Review of the Principal Trends in the Life of the Catholic Church in the United States,* issued by the National Conference of Catholic Bishops in 1974.

3. Archbishop Bartoletti, Secretary General of the Italian Episcopal Conference, speaking at the 1974 Synod of Roman Catholic Bishops. Quoted from *L'Osservatore Romano.*

4. Archbishop Roger Etchegaray at the 1974 Synod. Quoted from *L'Osservatore Romano.*

5. "Christ, the great Prophet, who proclaimed the kingdom of His Father by the testimony of His life and the power of His words, continually fulfills His prophetic office until His full glory is revealed. He does this not only through the hierarchy who teach in His name and with His authority, but also through the laity." *Dogmatic Constitution on the Church,* IV. 35. From *The Documents of Vatican II,* ed. Abbott and Gallagher (New York: The America Press, 1966) p. 61.

Appendix One
Some Biblical Passages Concerning Prophecy

I. In the Old Testament
   A. The "call" of the prophets
      —Sam. 3 (Samuel is called by God)
      —Isa. 6 (the vision of the heavenly court)
      —Am. 7:14-16 (Amos defines his prophesying on the basis of his call from God)
      —Jer. 1 (Jeremiah is called and given a prophetic commission)
      —Hos. 1:2 (Hosea begins his prophetic mission)
      —Ez. 1-3 (Ezekiel is called)
   B. Some prophetic experiences
      —Num. 12:6-8 (how God speaks to Moses and the prophets)
      —1 Kings 19 (Elijah on Mount Horeb)
      —Jer. 20:7-12 (Jeremiah tries to resist the prophetic spirit)
      —1 Sam. 10 (Saul is caught up in the prophetic spirit)
      —2 Kings 3:9-20 (Elisha "stirs up" the spirit through music)
   C. The identity of the prophet
      1. "Messenger of Yahweh"
         —Isa. 44:26
         —Hag. 1:13
         —Mal. 3:1
      In Old Testament Israel, a messenger was considered to represent the person of the one who sent him. Thus, he would speak in the first person when delivering his message. Several passages which exemplify this custom are: Gen. 45:9, Num. 22:16, 1 Kings 2:30, Isa. 37:3. It

was this custom which the prophets adopted in giving their message in the name of the Lord.

2. "Shepherds"
   —Jer. 17:16
   —Zech. 11:4
3. "Guardians"
   —Isa. 62:6 (Heb. 2:1)
4. Watchmen
   —Amos 3:4
   —Isa. 56:10
   —Jer. 6:17
   —Ez. 3:17 pass.

D. False prophecy
   —Deut. 18:9-22 (an early test of prophecy)
   —Deut. 13:1-22 (a refinement of the earlier test)
   —1 Kings 22 (Micaiah and the prophets who were possessed by a lying spirit)
   —Jer. 23:9-10 (Jeremiah denounces the false prophets)
   —Jer. 28 (Jeremiah battles the prophet Hananiah)
   —Ez. 13 (Ezekiel vs. false prophecy)
   —Ez. 12:21)28 (the importance of accepting true prophecy)
   —Am. 2:9-3:8 (the reliability of true prophecy). It is worth noting that the term "false prophets" does not appear in the Old Testament. The prophets, whether true or false, are referred to simply as "the prophets." Thus, some of Jeremiah's bitterest denunciations are aimed at "the prophets." In the Old Testament, someone who prophesied was simply a prophet. He may prophesy the word of the Lord, or he may prophesy lies, delusions, dreams of his own mind. In the New Testament we find the distinction between genuine and false prophets introduced.

E. Prophets as intercessors
   —1 Sam. 12:19, 23; 15:2

—2 Kings 19:1ff.
—Jer. 8:16; 42:2
F. The power of the prophetic word
   —2 Kings 4:11-17
   —2 Kings 4:42-44
   —Jer. 28:15-17
   —2 Kings 20:1-11
   —2 Kings 6:15-23
G. Other aspects of prophecy
   —Num. 11:24-30 (Moses prays that all might prophesy)
   —Joel 2 (God says that his people will all receive a spirit of prophecy)
   —Chron. 25:3 (prophecy in worship)
   —2 Sam. 12 (God convicts David of sin)
   —Isa. 38:1-6 (a conditional prophecy)

II. In the New Testament
   A. Prophetic incidents
      —Acts 11:27f. (Prophets at Antioch; Agabus predicts famine)
      —Acts 13:1f. (Paul and Barnabas given a mission)
      —Acts 15:32 (Judas and Silas at Antioch)
      —Acts 20:23f. (the prophets predict Paul's trials)
      —Acts 21:4f. (Paul warned about trouble at Jerusalem)
      —Acts 21:9f. (Phillip's daughters; Agabus warns Paul about Jerusalem)
      —1 Tim. 1:18; 4:14 (Timothy learns of a special gif through prophecy)
   B. Testing the prophets
      —Mt. 7:15-23 (you will know them by their fruits)
      —1 Jn. 4:1f. (how to tell the true prophet from the false)
      —1 Cor. 12:3 (no one can say "Jesus is Lord" except by the Holy Spirit)
      —1 Thess. 5:20 (do not despise prophecy, but test it)
   C. The prophets in the New Testament

—Rom. 12:3-8
—1 Cor. 12-14
—Eph. 4:11-12
—Eph. 2:20
—Eph. 3:4-6

The Use of the Term "Charismata" in the New Testament

A case can be made for an important distinction in usage between certain words which are commonly translated "gift" or "spiritual gift" in English versions of the New Testament. On the whole, such terms are not used in what we would call a "technical sense" in the New Testament. The New Testament is a collection of early Christian writings; they are not formal theology. They are not even intended always to be formal church documents. The letters of Paul in particular are informal writings. The best approach is to stand back and take a look at how words are used within the New Testament, and draw from their use what we can. Looking for formal distinctions and technical uses is worthwhile only if the author intentionally used words in a technical way.

Use of the term *charismata* or *charisma* is a case in point. This term is used in a wide variety of ways in such passages as Rom. 1:11; Rom. 5:15,16; Rom. 6:23; Rom. 11:29; 1 Cor. 7:7; 2 Cor. 1:11; Rom. 12:6; 1 Cor. 1:7; 12:4,9,28,30,31; 1 Pet. 4:10; 1 Tim. 1:18; 4:14; 2 Tim. 1:6. The meaning of the term covers in these passages everything from the divinely given ability to prophesy to the "gift" of a release from prison. Paul probably used this word with great frequency because he meant something by it—but meant something not in the technical sense of a precise and unvarying meaning, but rather of an aspect of the "gift" referred to, namely its wholly gratuitous character.

There is good reason for thinking, however, that within the broader range of uses Paul finds for this word, he has also a more specific, almost technical use. The word appears in every passage in the letters referring to the equipment given to individuals to suit them for a place in the body of Christ (with one exception, to which I will return in a moment). The word is used in this sense in Rom. 12:6, 1 Cor. 1:7; 12:4,9,28,30,31; 1 Pet. 4:10.

Each of these passages lists the gifts which enable individuals to take a place in the community. It is worth noting that the only place in which it appears outside of Paul in the New Testament is in 1 Pet. 4:10—where it is again used of gifts which fit one for a place of service in the community.

There is one other passage where such gifts are listed, Eph. 4:8. But this passage is a quotation from the Old Testament, and is probably not Paul's own choice for translating the passage. Another important word occurs in 1 Corinthians 12-14, *pneumatika*. The term means simply "spirituals," and the translation "spiritual gift" is an interpretation. Paul uses *pneumatika* in 1 Cor. 12:1 and 14:1, and nowhere else. If the distinction between these two Greek words is born in mind, the section in 1 Corinthians from chapter 12 through chapter 14 takes on a different light.

There are, Paul says, different gifts *(charismata)* in the body (12:4-30) of Christ, and each of us must be content with the place God has assigned us. If he has given us the gift to do one sort of service, then we ought to strive to serve as well as we can in that place. At the same time, there are "spirituals" *(pneumatika)* which are open to every member of the body, and which all can, in good conscience, seek after (14:1).

It is then possible to reconcile Paul's seemingly contradictory advice in chapter 12 (1-30) and 14:1. It is right and good to seek for the transitory spirituals *(pneumatika)* but not to strive for the gifts *(charismata)* which determine our place in the body. With these gifts, we should be content to receive what God assigns us. But what then of 12:31, where Paul seemingly exhorts us to seek the higher *charismata?*

Gerhard Iber presents an interpretation of 1 Cor. 12:31

which seems plausible, and which eliminates the seeming con-
tradictions in Paul's approach to the gifts. The Greek form of
the verb in this verse can be translated either in the indicative
or the imperative. Iber says that it does not seem likely Paul
would have intended it in the imperative in the light of his
foregoing admonition *not* to seek a different gift than you have
been given. He would therefore translate the passage as "You
are striving after the greatest gifts." The passage then con-
tinues. "But I will show you a more excellent way."

In 1 Cor. 12-14 then, Paul both encourages the Corinthian
church to seek after the "spirituals" but to be content with the
"gift" God has given us. Among the "gifts" one is not greater
than another, because all parts of the body are necessary and
important. But among the "spirituals" there is a difference in
value. Specifically, prophecy is more useful for building up the
body than is tongues (ch. 14). The way of love impels us both
to be content with our place in the community, neither being
puffed up with pride nor embittered through envy, and to seek
those "spirituals" which can most contribute to the good of
the whole.

The importance of this distinction in the use of the terms
charisma and *pneumatikon* as it applies to prophecy, has to do
with the recognition of prophets in the church. Paul says both
that many people can experience, and should seek to experience, the *pneumatikon* of prophecy—the transitory but legitimate and useful exercise of prophecy under inspiration upon
occasion. But no one should seek a *charisma* of prophecy, i.e.,
no one should seek to be a prophet. Prophets are prophets
because God has assigned them that *charisma*. His choice is
sovereign, not to be tampered with by the ambitions of men.
Furthermore, though the prophet exercises a powerful and
important gift (Paul consistently ranks them second after apostles) they are no more to be esteemed because of that gift than
anyone else in the body. Their *gift* should be esteemed, because through it the prophet brings to the community God's

word. But the person who bears the gift is of no more value than another man who bears a different gift. The gift has an intrinsic worth, and the man has an intrinsic worth. But the worth of the man is determined on the basis of his conformity to the character of God—on the basis of the perfection of his love—not on the basis of his possession of a gift. Of the gift he is only the steward, not the owner.

References

Kittel, Gerhard, *Theological Dictionary of the New Testament* (Grand Rapids, Michigan: Eerdmans, 1964).

Iber, Gerhard, "Zum Verstandnis von. 1 Korinther 12, 31," *Zeitschrift fur neutestamentliche Wissenschaft,* 1963, p. 43ff.

Clark, Stephen, "Words for 'Gift' in the New Testament," an unpublished paper.